The

Pug

An Owner's Guide To

A HAPPY HEALTHY PET

Howell Book House

Howell Book House
A Simon & Schuster Macmillan Company
1633 Broadway
New York, NY 10019

Library of Congress Cataloging-in-Publication Data
Patterson, Edward, 1917–
The pug: an owner's guide to a happy, healthy pet/Edward Patterson.
p. cm.

ISBN: 0-87605-496-3

1. Pug.   I. Title.
SF429.P9P38   1996
636.7'6—dc20   96-22140
                              CIP

Manufactured in the United States of America
10 9 8 7

Series Director: Dominique De Vito
Series Assistant Director: Ariel Cannon
Book Design: Michele Laseau
Cover Design: Iris Jeromnimon
Illustration: Jeff Yesh
Photography:
  Cover photos by Paulette Braun/Pets by Paulette
  Joan Balzarini: 96
  Mary Bloom: 96, 136, 145
  Paulette Braun/Pets by Paulette: 2-3, 7, 9, 11, 19, 20, 23, 24, 34-35, 41, 51, 56, 92, 96
  Buckinghamhill American Cocker Spaniels: 148
  Sian Cox: 25, 39, 57, 134
  Dr. Ian Dunbar: 98, 101, 103, 111, 116–117, 122, 123, 127
  Andrew Giangola: 26
  Dan Lyons: 96
  Cathy Merrithew: 129
  Liz Palika: 133
  Edward and Charlotte Patterson: 27, 28, 36, 37, 58
  Cheryl Primeau: 48, 59, 60
  Susan Rezy: 18, 96–97
  Judith Strom: 53, 66, 75, 96, 107, 110, 128, 130, 135, 137, 139, 140, 144, 149, 150
  Faith Uridel: 5, 8, 62, 67
  Jean Wentworth: 42, 46, 84
Production Team: Kathleen Caulfield, Trudy Coler, Vic Peterson, Jama Carter, and Troy Barnes

Contents

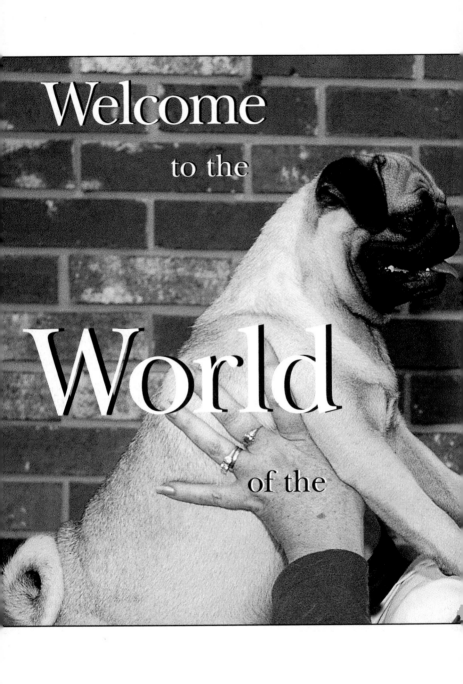

Welcome

to the

World

of the

part one

Pug

External Features of the Pug

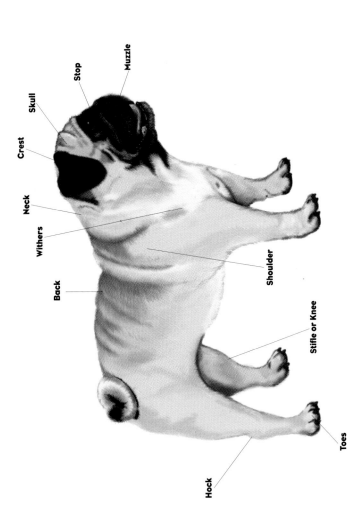

chapter 1

What
Is a
Pug?

Oh, lovely and most charming Pug
Thy graceful air and heavenly mug
The beauties of your mind do shine
And every bit is shaped so fine
Your tail is most divine.

—Marjorie Fleming

This little nineteenth-century poem, penned by a very young English lady, Marjorie Fleming, shortly before her death at the age of eight, tells us with admirable simplicity what a Pug can mean to its owner.

But what exactly is a Pug? What makes a Pug so unique, so different from a Boston Terrier, a Pekingese, or a French Bulldog?

The Standard

In 1885, an American standard for the Pug was composed. This standard describes the *ideal* Pug. No animal actually lives up to the standard in every way, but breeders keep trying to come as close to this description as possible.

The Pug standard is closely copied from one previously written by the Kennel Club in England. Since 1885, a few additions have been made by the Pug Dog Club of America and approved by the American Kennel Club (AKC), but the original standard is basically unchanged.

In the following discussion of the Pug Dog standard, the official AKC standard appears in italics. The author's comments follow in regular type. (For a copy of the complete standard, write to the Pug Dog Club of America. See page 33 for the address.)

General Appearance

Symmetry and general appearance are decidedly square and cobby.

A Pug is square. Not literally, of course, but when we look at a Pug from any angle we should get an impression of squareness. The height at the shoulders should be about the same distance as the length from the front of his chest to the rear.

SIZE, PROPORTION, SUBSTANCE

The Pug should be multum in parvo *and this condensation of form . . . is shown by compactness of form, well knit proportions and hardness of developed muscle.*

Multum in parvo is a Latin phrase every Pug owner should know. Translated freely, it means that there

---

WHAT IS A BREED STANDARD?

A breed standard—a detailed description of an individual breed—is meant to portray the *ideal* specimen of that breed. This includes ideal structure, temperament, gait, type—all aspects of the dog. Because the standard describes an ideal specimen, it isn't based on any particular dog. It is a concept against which judges compare actual dogs and breeders strive to produce dogs. At a dog show, the dog that wins is the one that comes closest, in the judge's opinion, to the standard for its breed. Breed standards are written by the breed parent clubs, the national organizations formed to oversee the well-being of the breed. They are voted on and approved by the members of the parent clubs.

is a great deal in a little package—a compact, well-proportioned little dog with a big heart.

HEAD

The head is large, massive, round. The eyes are dark in color, very large, bold and prominent.

The Pug's crowning glory is the head, round when viewed in profile, square when viewed from the front. Velvety black ears fall to about eye level. The large, round, dark eyes look at you in a soft, pleading, quizzical way, but come alive with excitement during playtime. The muzzle is broad, to match the breadth of the skull and, when his mouth is closed, you should see neither teeth nor tongue. Best of all are the wrinkles around the face, covering his brow and looping over his black nose, contributing so much to his characteristic expression.

In a dog show, a Pug is judged on how closely he conforms to the breed standard.

NECK, TOPLINE, BODY

The neck is strong and thick with enough length to carry the head proudly. The short back is level from the withers to the high tail set. The body is cobby, wide in chest and well ribbed up.

This is self-explanatory when you look at a correct Pug. The "withers" are the shoulders, and "cobby" means compact.

FOREQUARTERS

The legs are very strong, straight, of moderate length, and are set well under. The shoulders are moderately laid back.

7

Standing in front of our Pug, we see straight, sturdy legs coming down from broad shoulders and chest, forming a square. We do not want to see a bowed front and feet turned outward like a Bulldog.

A Pug's body should give the overall impression of being square.

Moving around to the side of our Pug, we see a broad, strong neck curving slightly just behind the skull and merging smoothly into the shoulders. The legs should be directly under the shoulders and the full, rounded chest should protrude well forward of the legs. The topline, from shoulders to tail, should be straight and level, the tail set high and curled tightly over either hip. The rear legs should look strong, and when viewed from the side, be moderately bent and parallel to each other when viewed from the rear. The buttocks should be broad, emphasizing the dog's squareness even when viewed from above.

COAT

The coat is fine, smooth, short and glossy, neither hard nor woolly.

In either color—black or fawn—the Pug's coat should be short and should feel smooth and soft to the touch, neither hard nor coarse.

COLOR

The colors are silver, apricot-fawn or black. The silver or apricot-fawn colors should be decided so as to make the contrast complete between the color and the trace and the mask.

Pugs usually come in one of two colors: black and fawn. Black Pugs should have a shiny, jet-black coat and very dark eyes. Occasionally, you will see a white mark or blaze on the chest or paws. This is considered a "mismark" and is inherited from a strain of black Pugs originating in China. Although it is not preferable, it does not affect the overall beauty of the dog. Fawns also will occasionally have a white mark but, as it more easily blends into the lighter coat, it is much less apparent. Except for color, there should be no difference

Black Pugs are not uncommon, though fawn Pugs outnumber them by ten to one.

between black and fawn Pugs. Fawns do outnumber blacks to a considerable degree, perhaps as much as ten to one.

One factor that may account for the popularity of the fawn over the black Pug is the fawn's markings. Its muzzle is—or should be—jet black, as should its ears, the moles on its cheeks and its nails. Most desirable also is a darkened spot centered on the forehead known as a thumbmark or diamond. The line between the black muzzle and the lighter colored upper face should be quite distinct.

The rolls of skin that form along the neck and throat are a distinctive feature of the Pug, though the standard makes no mention of them.

The chin and muzzle of most Pugs will begin graying anywhere between two and six years of age.

The standard also mentions a silver coat, a color which has become quite rare in the United States, though perhaps less so elsewhere. A silver coat has been compared to the color of moonlight, in contrast to the sunlike color of the true fawn. Silver is devoid of any brightness. There is a tendency to confuse silver with smutty fawn.

THE AMERICAN KENNEL CLUB

Familiarly referred to as "the AKC," the American Kennel Club is a nonprofit organization devoted to the advancement of purebred dogs. The AKC maintains a registry of recognized breeds and adopts and enforces rules for dog events including shows, obedience trials, field trials, hunting tests, lure coursing, herding, earthdog trials, agility and the Canine Good Citizen program. It is a club of clubs, established in 1884 and composed, today, of over 500 autonomous dog clubs throughout the United States. Each club is represented by a delegate; the delegates make up the legislative body of the AKC, voting on rules and electing directors. The American Kennel Club maintains the Stud Book, the record of every dog ever registered with the AKC, and publishes a variety of materials on purebred dogs, including a monthly magazine, books and numerous educational pamphlets. For more information, contact the AKC at the address listed in Chapter 13, "Resources," and look for the names of their publications in Chapter 12, "Recommended Reading."

LOOSE SKIN

Pugs generally have loose skin that sometimes forms rolls of flesh around the throat, over the shoulders and down the back. These rolls usually become more pronounced with advancing age. The standard makes no mention of this phenomenon; some people like it, some don't.

We have now described what a Pug looks like standing still—which rarely happens. So, how should they look while in motion?

GAIT

Viewed from the front, the forelegs should be carried well forward, showing no weaknesss in the pasterns, the paws landing squarely with the central toes straight ahead.

As we watch a Pug move toward us, his legs should swing forward freely with each one moving in a straight line, not swinging out or tending to cross while moving. When he is moving away from us, again the legs should move parallel to one another, along the same line as the front legs, and should not swing out or in. As his trot picks up and he moves faster, there is a tendency for the legs to move toward a center line, and this is quite proper.

Of course, it is not at all unusual for a Pug—especially a puppy—to move at full gallop, with ears and tail streaming behind. This exhibits the Pug's enthusiasm at its best, high spirits, the sheer joy of being alive, the excitement of rough play.

It doesn't matter if your pet Pug doesn't fit all the requirements of the standard. He will still be a loving pet.

TEMPERAMENT

This is an even-tempered breed, exhibiting stability, playfulness, great charm, dignity and an outgoing loving disposition.

This description of the Pug's temperament sums up the breed's all-around appeal. What does the Pug Dog Club of America have to say about the breed?

No other dog can equal the Pug in his virtues as a family pet. He appeals to Mother because of his natural cleanliness, intelligence, and the fact that he is a "Toy." He appeals to Father because he is a husky, sturdy dog with very little upkeep, needing no professional grooming. Children adore Pugs and Pugs adore children. They are not too delicate for fun and games. Older people and shut-ins find them perfect as companions because their greatest need is to be by your side and accepted into your way of life. . . . A Pug is anxious to please, anxious to learn, and anxious to love. His biggest requirement is that you love him back. . . . The Pug's place is in the Toy Group. It is the largest breed in that Group. It is not so much a Toy because of his size but rather because of his nature. You can see by his history that for many centuries he has been bred to be a companion and a pleasure to his owner.

A pet Pug may not live up to all the requirements of the Standard. And yet with the right temperament, attitude and good nature he will be a joy to you and your family.

chapter 2

The
Pug's
Ancestry

The history of many breeds can be precisely traced back to an original homeland or even to an original breeder. The Pug is an exception and let us say from the beginning that the early "history" of this unusual, short-faced dog is more conjecture than established fact.

Champion Wolf's Li'l Joe

An Ancient Breed

Over the years, many people have theorized that the Pug is descended from the Mastiff or from the Bulldog. However, it is now generally accepted that the Pug is as close to an original breed as possible. Descriptions of the Pug from China date back as far as 1000 B.C.

In that era, Pugs were the house pets of emperors and nobility. One Chinese ruler was said to have named a Pug as his viceroy, while another endowed his favorite Pug with a high literary title. It is a known fact that Pug-like dogs were given as gifts of great value to Japanese rulers, and several were presented to Russia's first ambassador to China. Beginning in the late sixteenth century, when trade was established with Europe, Portuguese, Dutch, Spanish and English sailors brought some Pugs back to their home countries.

THE PUG IN EUROPE

It was in the Netherlands that the Pug first gained wide popularity in the West. Legend has it that during

the Spanish attempt to gain control over Holland, the Spanish troops launched a surprise attack on the Dutch camp, whose army was headed by William the Silent of the House of Orange. William's Pug was the first to alert his master to the attack, before any sentinel, and was credited with saving William's life. After that incident, the Pug became the honored pet of the Dutch ruling house. In 1688 when William of Orange became king of England, his retinue arrived in London with a large assemblage of Pugs.

Champion Sabbaday Opus displays the Pug's winning charm.

Other early Pugs in Europe are known through the paintings of England's William Hogarth, and Spain's Francisco Goya. Hogarth pictured one Pug as quite small and black, definitely identifiable as the true Pug we know today. He also portrayed a larger Pug with a longer muzzle and long legs, indicating the probability of cross-breeding with another unidentified breed. Goya's famous painting of the Duchess of Alba portrays a fawn-colored Pug that would be quite proper by today's standard.

Early in the nineteenth century, the popularity of the Pug seems to have faded. At the same time, dog fanciers began to experiment with cross-breeding in order to establish or reinforce desirable characteristics in their breeds. For example, Pugs were supposedly interbred with Bulldogs in an effort to shorten the Bulldog's muzzle. The French are believed to have crossed Pugs with Bulldogs to reduce the latter's size, resulting in the French Bulldog. Almost surely, the Pug was bred into the Brussels Griffon. Other, often indiscriminate, cross-breeding did much damage to the breed and resulted in a large number of ugly, nondescript dogs that we see depicted in nineteenth-century paintings and engravings, barely recognizable as Pugs.

Pugs have not always been held in high esteem. Toward the end of the eighteenth century, the breed's popularity reached a low ebb. Wrote one author in 1804:

> In the whole catalogue of the canine species, there is not one of less utility, or possessing less the powers of attraction than the Pug dog, applicable to no sport, appropriated to no useful purpose, susceptible of no predominant passion, and in no way whatever remarkable for any extra eminence, he has continued from era to era for what alone he might have been originally intended, the patient follower of a ruminating philosopher, or the adulating and consolatory companion of an old maid.

WHERE DID DOGS COME FROM?

It can be argued that dogs were right there at man's side from the beginning of time. As soon as human beings began to document their own existence, the dog was among their drawings and inscriptions. Dogs were not just friends, they served a purpose: There were dogs to hunt birds, pull sleds, herd sheep, burrow after rats—even sit in laps! What your dog was originally bred to do influences the way it behaves. The American Kennel Club recognizes over 140 breeds, and there are hundreds more distinct breeds around the world. To make sense of the breeds, they are grouped according to their size or function. The AKC has seven groups:

1) Sporting, 2) Working,
3) Herding, 4) Hounds,
5) Terriers, 6) Toys,
7) Non-Sporting

Can you name a breed from each group? Here's some help: (1) Golden Retriever; (2) Doberman Pinscher; (3) Collie; (4) Beagle; (5) Scottish Terrier; (6) Maltese; and (7) Dalmatian. All modern domestic dogs (*Canis familiaris*) are related, however different they look, and are all descended from *Canis lupus*, the gray wolf.

**FAMOUS
OWNERS OF
THE PUG**

Sammy Davis Jr.

Andy Warhol

Lena Horne

Duke and
Duchess of
Windsor

Prince Ranier
and Princess
Grace of
Monaco

In rebuttal, another author wrote: "No doubt the habit of many old ladies of giving Pugs no exercise, and at the same time cramming them with food until their goggles popped (and Pugs will never stop eating so long as anything edible is within reach) contributed to the unfair impression that all dogs of this breed were fat, immobile, pop-eyed, snorting slugs . . ." Today there is little contention that the Pug is a companion dog *par excellence.*

It should be noted that, even after the popularity of the Pugs declined sharply between 1800 and 1850, a number of devoted breeders continued to rear them and make every effort to improve the breed and halt the trend toward mongrelization. With the introduction of Pug imports from China in the latter half of the century, the fortunes of the breed began a sharp upswing. In fact, it could truly be said that the history of the Pug we know today really began at this point, as dog shows were begun and breeders began to keep better records.

THE BLACK PUG

Although black Pugs existed in England concurrently with the fawns, they were generally not held in favor and, in fact, were often "culled" from the litter and the less said about them, the better. In his 1730 painting, "The House of Cards," the painter Hogarth depicted a black Pug, so we know that some of them escaped.

Queen Victoria was also known to have owned a black Pug, one heavily marked with white, indicating that it was probably of Chinese origin. But it was not until 1886 that blacks were taken seriously and placed in competition with the fawns. For this, we must thank the well-born English Lady Brassey, a lover of Pugs and an inveterate world traveler. While yachting in Chinese waters in 1876, she acquired and brought back to England several black Pugs, who made a considerable impact on the gene pool in that country. Furthermore, Lady Brassey had the temerity to exhibit her Chinese blacks at a dog show in 1886, where they gained instant popularity, leading to the creation of several kennels specializing in blacks, as well as to interbreeding with fawns, a practice still in existence.

THE CHINESE INFLUENCE

The Pugs that we know today are most likely the descendants of fresh blood brought into England from China in the mid- to late 1800s. At this point the written and graphic record of the breed begins to have some historical accuracy.

In 1860 British troops sacked the Imperial Palace in Beijing. This event brought fresh imports of Pugs, Pekingese and, to a lesser extent, Japanese Chins (until recently known as Japanese Spaniels) to the West.

Twentieth-century Pugs, including Champion Hazelbridge Frog, have been influenced by imports of Pugs from China in the late nineteenth century.

About this time, the Chinese Empress Tsu Hsi brought the art and science of breeding to an all-time high, complete with detailed breeding records. The records clearly distinguish between the longer-legged, short-coated Lo-sze (Pug) and the short-legged, long-coated Pekingese. The following description was written by Wang Hou-Chun, one of the imperial kennel supervisors:

17

One of the most important characteristics of the Chinese Lo-sze is, in addition to universal shortness of coat, elasticity of skin existing to a greater degree than with the "Pekingese." The point most sought after by Chinese breeders was the "Prince" mark, formed by the wrinkles on the forehead with a vertical bar in imitation of the Chinese character for *Prince.* . . . The button, or white blaze on the forehead was also encouraged in the Lo-sze dog, but was not of the same importance as the wrinkles. Other points, such as compactness of body, flatness of face, squareness of jaw and soundness of bone, are similar to those of the "Pekingese," except as regards the ears, which were small and likened to a dried half-apricot set with the outer face on the side of the head and pointing slightly backward. The "horn-ear" [which we can equate to the modern Pug's "rose" ear] is also admissible. The legs are but slightly bent at the elbow. The tail is docked . . . with a view to symmetrical form. The curly tail, however, is known to have existed, and the double curl was also known.

Pugs like this one have endeared themselves to their owners for centuries.

Although we are unable to date this description of a Pug, it most certainly preceded the first British standard for the Pug (1883), and may well be the first defining description of the breed. Tail docking was *never* practiced in the West.

PUGS IN THE UNITED STATES

When Pugs arrived in the United States is a matter of conjecture; few records exist prior to 1879, when some twenty-four of them were exhibited in New York.

In America, the Pug's popularity has increased steadily since the 1950s.

While quite popular in the early years of this century, the Pug's popularity waned severely during and after World War I, but began a slow but steady revival when, in 1931, the Pug Dog Club of America was established and became a member of the American Kennel Club. However, it was not until 1953 that we find any written record of the PDC's activities. From then on, the breed has increased steadily in popularity.

WHY THE NAME "PUG"?

Why do we call them Pugs? In the Far East, they were variously known as Lao-tze, Foo dogs and Pai dogs. In German-speaking countries, they were know as Mopshonden, Mops or Mopsi. The French know them as Carlin, the Italians as Carlini. Only the English-speaking countries call them Pugs.

Some say the word derives from the Latin *pugnus,* meaning fist, because the Pug's head, viewed from the side, resembles a clenched fist. A more likely origin was the English use of the word "pug" in past centuries as a term of endearment. It was often applied to pet monkeys during the nineteenth century, when most ladies of quality had such pets upon whom they most likely lavished more love and care than on their own children. A lady might even refer fondly to her husband as "my dear Pug." The dogs, with their somewhat monkeylike expressions, were thus referred to not as "Pugs" but as "Pug dogs," thus distinguishing them from monkeys and husbands. In course of time, the dogs became known simply as "Pugs."

Pugs may have gotten their name from the Latin word pugnus, *meaning "fist," because that's what their heads look like.*

Famous Pugs

As I mentioned earlier, the House of Orange had a great affection for Pugs, as one of them reportedly saved the life of William of Orange. When, in 1688, William's grandson, William III, mounted the British throne with his wife, Mary, the couple brought with them quite a few Pugs, leading to that breed's great popularity in England. One even appeared in a formal portrait of George III.

Another famous (or infamous) Pug was Fortune, whose beautiful owner, the Empress Josephine, kept him with her at all times—including her wedding night! When Napoléon approached his bride, he covered that she was sharing her bed with Fortune. Fortune welcomed this intruder by taking a piece out of his leg.

In more recent times, Pugs have been owned by such notable persons as the Duke and Duchess of Windsor and the famous film actress, Sylvia Sidney.

The Pug Today

Today, the Pug is renowned as a superb companion. He is a recognized charmer in the print media and on television, and a companion to famous faces all over the world. But the Pug's achievements do not stop there.

PUGS IN OBEDIENCE

Though the Pug has a reputation for being stubborn, he is also loyal, curious and intelligent. These latter traits serve him well in obedience training and competition. Though, admittedly, the Pug is a rarer breed in the obedience ring than, for example, a German Shepherd, many Pugs have proven their worth in obedience events.

Whether or not you intend to compete in organized activities, obedience training is helpful for every Pug, and should be started informally when your Pug is a puppy. Start with easy exercises, offer lots of praise and positive reinforcement, and you will soon find your Pug wants to be a part of this fun activity. For more information on obedience work, talk to your vet or breeder, or contact one of the related organizations listed in Chapter 9, "Resources."

THERAPY PUGS

Obedience training will make your Pug better behaved and more responsive in every kind of situation. This will be especially useful if you plan to try other activities with your Pug, like therapy work. All over the country, organizations have been established to bring the love, affection and attention that pets offer to those who need it most. People who cannot keep pets with them because they live in an institutional environment, such as a nursing home, benefit from visits by therapy animals. A Pug's easy-going temperament, friendly nature, and huggable, unintimidating size make him a perfect candidate for this kind of work.

chapter 3

The **World**

According to the

Pug

For thousands of years, the Pug has been bred for the sole purpose of being a companion. He does not track, hunt, retrieve, point or herd. He loves. And he is happiest when he is loved in return. Few today will argue with the statement that the Pug is the companion *par excellence.*

Pugs are marvelously adaptive and are anxious to discover and share your mood. They love to run loose (always in an enclosed area), to snooze in front of the fireplace or romp in the snow.

The Multi-Talented Pug

From rough play in the backyard or a tramp in the woods, to a gentle guardian of an infant or a patient listener to one's problems, the Pug can be all things to all people. His protective instincts, while well known, never lead to aggressiveness. His fondness for children of all ages and his reliability as a companion to man are legendary. Further, it is our unshakable belief that an additional purpose for which this

breed was cultivated was to keep master and mistress warm during the long winter nights of interior China's winters.

As you walk through your home, you will hear the "click, click, click" of your Pug's toenails as he follows close at your heels, wondering what you will do next: go to

Pugs thrive on attention and affection.

the kitchen for a little snack, sit in your favorite armchair to watch TV or read a book, or go for a walk to see what's new in the neighborhood. Any one of these events (or a dozen others) will send your Pug into an active explosion of joy.

Arguably, he could be called a guard dog for, while he will never attack an intruder, he will certainly give voice when a stranger is approaching, but will seldom bark for no reason at all.

Pugs Are Social Dogs

They are not "one-person" dogs. They will know who is a member of their family and will gladly share the company of any family member with the time to spare for them. They may, however, display some partiality toward the one who puts down the food dish.

Pugs Like Routine

They like routine. If you take them for a walk each morning, they will come to expect this every day. If they receive some daily grooming, they will look forward to it.

A Pug wants to know what is expected of him. Will he share you or your child's bed at night, or will he sleep in his very own place in the kitchen or laundry room? Is he supposed to bark at strangers or simply go to the front door as a stranger approaches the house? At what hour can he expect dinner? Will he beg at the family's dinner table or take a snooze while his humans eat? These are a few of the things your pug will want to know for, above all, he wishes to please his people. The way to make your Pug happiest is to train him well so he knows what to expect and when to expect it. Establish a schedule and stick to it. This will make your Pug comfortable and secure that all his needs are being met by the people he loves and trusts.

Pugs are eager to participate in your life and share your moods.

Pugs Need Attention
The worst thing that can happen to a Pug is to be ignored. Once they get used to your routines, they will want to share in them as much as possible. They will want to be with you whether you are resting, walking, driving or washing dishes. Of course, they cannot share many of your activities, but will soon learn which are which.

Grooming Requirements
If they are kept clean by frequent brushing and occasional bathing, they are largely free from doggy odors.

Any bad odors they emit are probably caused by either flatulence or bad breath. Flatulence could mean that they are not being fed the right food (see Chapter 5).

Bad breath is most often the result of tartar collecting on the teeth, and is a sign that a good cleaning by your veterinarian is in order. Teeth should be checked by your vet at least every six months, and failure to do so will result not only in unpleasant breath, but also premature loss of teeth and the discomfort of dental abscesses.

With a minimal amount of grooming, your Pug will be stylish and beautiful.

Although this is a short-coated breed, the length and density of the coat will vary considerably from dog to dog. Most fawn Pugs have double coats: a layer of very soft undercoat, under a layer of longer and harsher coat. Puppies in particular will normally have a very dense undercoat; and, as they mature, much of this will be shed. Older dogs also shed, sometimes seasonally, sometimes more often. If the outer coat sheds, this is often a sign of some other health problem and, if severe, calls for a check-up by your vet. Black Pugs are usually (but not always) single-coated, lacking the soft undercoat. For that reason, they shed less than the fawns.

Pugs Snore

As in any other breed with a short muzzle, Pugs tend to emit a variety of noises when they doze or sleep. This can vary from a slight snuffling to a good, hearty snore. The test of a true Pug lover is how he reacts to this snoring. Some find it annoying, but the Pug lover is comforted by the sound, knowing that as long as the snoring is regular, everything is all right.

Pugs Need Exercise

A Pug is by nature both an active dog and a "lounge lizard"—whichever you teach him to be. Either way, he should engage in daily exercise to remain in good health. A daily walk of about a mile or so is one way to accomplish this, and at least a portion of this should be at a brisk pace.

If you have two or more Pugs and an enclosure around your property, chances are the Pugs will exercise each other—and few things are more fun to watch than two or more Pugs chasing each other at full tilt, mouths open, ears flying and tails trying to catch up with the rest of the dogs' bodies.

Quite obviously, the degree of exercise will be governed by the weather to some extent. Over 80 or 85 degrees, exercise must be modified; likewise, when the temperature drops below 45 degrees, your Pug should not be left outside for extended periods, even if you have provided him with a sweater. When left outside, a Pug should always have water and, in hot weather, available shade.

Like other short-muzzled breeds, Pugs snore when they snooze. To the true Pug lover, this is a beautiful noise!

Unlike people, dogs do not perspire over their entire body, but are cooled by panting and through the pads of their feet. Hence, they are more susceptible to heat stroke than are people. Because Pugs are bracycephalic, or short muzzled, they can overheat even more easily. If you live in a hot climate, exercise your Pug in the early morning or evening. Never leave your

Two or more Pugs will exercise each other in an enclosed area.

Pug in the car on a hot day, even with the windows down. A stationary car can become too hot very quickly, and it's just not worth risking your Pug's life for a ride.

Nuisance Traits

Pugs have traits common to dogs of any breed that can be a nuisance. A male will typically want to "establish his territory" by lifting his leg here and there so that all intruding dogs will know who owns the house. And like all dogs, especially puppies, some Pugs like to chew on things and must be taught the difference between acceptable chewing material (such as ham bones, nylon toys and dog biscuits) and unacceptable material (such as furniture, carpet fringe and pillows).

If you have both a male and female, the male may "ride" the female in an effort either to breed her or demonstrate his dominance. This tendency can be greatly reduced, if not entirely eliminated, by having the male neutered and the female spayed. Spaying the female is desirable to avoid the need to isolate her during her heat cycles (about every six months) and to keep her from staining furniture with menstrual blood. (See Chapter 7 for complete information on spaying and neutering.)

Once you have lived with a Pug, it is hard to remember what life was like without one—even if you have had other breeds before. And if, once you bring one home, it occurs to you that two would be twice as good, then you are probably hooked for life.

The Peripatetic Pug

As I have mentioned throughout, your Pug wants to be with you wherever you go. When you travel, your Pug will certainly want to come along, and if your travel plans can accommodate him, you will most likely want to bring him along.

TRAVELING BY CAR

If you are traveling by car, you will be using a safety belt in case of accidents. Of course your Pug cannot wear one, so you have to take other measures to keep your Pug safe in a moving vehicle. Unless he is in a firmly anchored crate, he will be unprotected. Use either a wire crate or an airline-type plastic crate; the wire crate allows for somewhat better air circulation, an important thing to think about in the Pug's case, while the plastic crate is lighter and easier to clean. Whichever type of crate you choose, make sure it is held in place by a couple of elastic straps (bungee cords) so that, in the event of an accident or sudden stop, the crate will not be hurled through the

> **CHARACTERISTICS OF THE PUG**
>
> good with children
>
> very social
>
> tends to snore loudly
>
> does not require intense exercise
>
> adaptable
>
> cannot tolerate extreme heat

air. The ideal placement of the crate is on the rear deck of a station wagon or minivan. In a sedan, either remove the rear seat cushion and secure the crate there, or place the crate on top of the rear seat cushion with some object (e.g., a rolled-up towel) placed under the crate to level it. A wire crate will require a galvanized metal tray on the bottom (in case of an "accident"). Over the tray, or in the bottom of an airline crate, should be placed either towels or newspaper, with spare supplies available just in case. A water cup and cup holder should also be placed in the crate.

Supplies to be brought along, in addition to enough food for the trip, include bottled water, extra towels or newspaper, a roll of paper towels, a package of sandwich bags or a "pooper scooper," a lead, and finally a can of deodorant spray. En route and after you arrive at your destination, Pugsy will need to be taken for a walk and exercised. Good manners demand that you clean up after him. Hence, the pooper scooper and sandwich bags. To use the latter, turn the bag inside out, insert your hand inside the bag, scoop up, then slip your hand out of the bag while reversing it so it is rightside-up. Zip it up and throw it in the nearest trash receptacle.

If you are staying in a hotel or motel, you might also bring a sheet of polyurethane or an old shower curtain, spread it out in a draft free part of the room, and place your Pug's crate on top of it. This will catch any food or water spill (or anything else) and keep you off the hotel's blacklist.

If you are traveling in cold weather, be sure to bring a coat or jacket for Pugsy. If the weather is likely to be hot, you must take steps to be sure he remains cool. Inside his traveling crate, a couple of sealed bottles of frozen blue ice can be placed under his towel, and, for walking, he may be fitted with an ice collar. Pharmacies usually carry elongated rubber bottles designed to be filled with hot water or ice and wrapped around the neck. Filled with cracked or shaved ice, they will fit around Pugsy's neck and keep his temperature down. Should he become overheated, remove the ice collar and place it against

A DOG'S SENSES

Sight: With their eyes located farther apart than ours, dogs can detect movement at a greater distance than we can, but they can't see as well up close. They can also see better in less light, but can't distinguish many colors.

Sound: Dogs can hear about four times better than we can, and they can hear high-pitched sounds especially well. Their ancestors, the wolves, howled to let other wolves know where they were; our dogs do the same, but they have a wider range of vocalizations, including barks, whimpers, moans and whines.

Smell: A dog's nose is his greatest sensory organ. His sense of smell is so great he can follow a trail that's weeks old, detect odors diluted to one-millionth the concentration we'd need to notice them, even sniff out a person under water!

Taste: Dogs have fewer taste buds than we do, so they're likelier to try anything—and usually do, which is why it's especially important for their owners to monitor their food intake. Dogs are omnivores, which means they eat meat as well as vegetable matter like grasses and weeds.

Touch: Dogs are social animals and love to be petted, groomed and played with.

his anal area, and place the blue ice under his feet. If this does not cool him down quickly, he should be soaked in water or placed in a tub or picnic chest filled with water or ice. Offer water to drink if he will accept it.

AIR TRAVEL

If Pugsy will travel with you by air, an airline crate is a must. Any crate that allows him to stand up and turn around, with no aperture so large that a foot or tail could protrude is acceptable. You may ship him as accompanied freight for a small additional fee, in which case he will travel in a pressurized cargo compartment whose temperature should be maintained at approximately the same level as the passenger cabin. Some airlines will allow small animals to be taken into the cabin with their owner and placed under the seat. The airline must approve this in advance, and the carrier must be fairly rigid and no larger than any other carry on luggage. Pugs are usually a bit large for carriers this small, but it has been our experience that airlines are inclined to overlook this. The Pug will be a bit cramped, but if a flight is less than four hours, your Pug will tolerate this confinement as long as he is with you and can hear your voice. This is the most preferable way to bring Pugsy with you for, in an emergency, he can be taken out for a short period. (Don't ask the flight attendant's permission!)

If he is traveling alone, Pugsy can be shipped as cargo. This is to be avoided if there is any change of aircraft en route, and should be done only if someone is waiting for him at his destination. Many airlines offer a special service for unaccompanied pets, for which they will charge an extra fee. It is worth using this option, for you can then leave the dog at the ticket counter where he will be kept cool (or warm), be the last loaded and the first to be unloaded, and be delivered directly to the ticket counter at the other end, thus avoiding a wait in the cargo area.

If You Have to Leave Your Pug

There will doubtless be times when it is impossible to fit a dog into your travel plans. In these cases, you will have to arrange for someone to care for your Pug.

KENNELS

This is the most popular option for pet owners when they must leave behind their animal friends. Ask your vet, breeder or groomer for a recommendation, and follow up by checking out the facilities yourself. Look for a clean kennel with both an inside and outside concrete run for your pet to exercise in. Make sure the kennel requires proof of shots, including one for kennel cough. There should be an attendant on the premises twenty four hours a day. Make sure the staff seems attentive and genuinely interested in your pet's specific needs.

IN-HOME PET CARE

This method of pet care has several advantages. Your pet will be able to remain in his home, in a familiar environment, and receive one-on-one attention. He will not be exposed to fleas or germs from other dogs, as he would in a kennel environment. However, there are drawbacks as well. Your Pug may be lonely and unhappy, and may take to chewing things or being otherwise destructive in your absence. Also, do you mind giving a stranger access to your home while you are away? Again, ask a trusted authority for recommendations about in-home care personnel. Meet with the person beforehand and introduce him or her to the dog. Don't settle for someone you aren't comfortable with.

Whenever you leave your Pug, do your part to ensure his comfort before you leave. See if you can get a friend or relative to play with him or walk him a few times a week. If your Pug will be boarding at the kennel, take along a few favorite toys. Leave detailed instructions with whomever will be caring for your Pug. In case of emergency, make sure to provide your vet's telephone number and a number at which you can be reached.

MORE INFORMATION ON PUGS

NATIONAL BREED CLUB

Pug Dog Club of America, Inc.
15457 Clover Ridge Dr.
Chesterfield, MO 63017

The club can send you information on the breed itself as well as the names and locations of local dog clubs or Pug Dog clubs in your area. Inquire about membership.

BOOKS

McBrearly, Joan McDonald. *The Book of the Pug.* Neptune City, NJ: TFH Publications, 1980.

Thomas, Shirley. *The New Pug.* New York: Howell Book House, 1990.

Vriends, Matthew. *Pugs.* Hauppage, NY: Barron's, 1994.

VIDEOS

American Kennel Club. *Pugs.*

Living

with a

part two

Pug

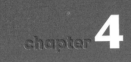
Bringing Your
Pug
Home

In the next several chapters, we will discuss how to take care of your Pug. When we buy a new automobile, we expect to get an owner's manual that tells us how to take care of our shiny new car—when to change the oil, how to drive it for maximum performance. A reputable Pug breeder should provide the buyer with similar information, and the conscientious new owner will study these instructions with care. For those who didn't get an "owner's manual" with their new Pug, we hope the following chapters will provide the information you need.

Initially, we would like to talk about bringing home a Pug puppy, leaving aside for the moment what to do when bringing a mature Pug into your home for the first time. But before you do either, ask yourself . . .

Are You Ready for a Pug?

Impulse-buying is usually a mistake; impulse-buying a puppy could be a disaster. We receive many calls from people who say, "I want a Pug." When questioned, they will sometimes admit that they know nothing about the breed except that "they are so cute." They have no fenced or protected area for a dog; they are planning to get married or move away; and everyone in the household works from nine to five, leaving a dog alone in the home. Yet such people will often want a Pug, and want it *today!*

Remember, you are taking on an additional member of the family who will require nourishment, medical care, and thoughtful attention for approximately thirteen years.

Make sure your Pug will have company and companionship during the day. If the members

of your family are not at home during the day, try to come home at lunchtime, let your puppy out and spend some time with her. If this isn't possible, try to get a neighbor or friend who lives close by to come spend time with the puppy. Your Pug thrives on human attention and guidance, and a puppy left alone most of the day will find ways to get your attention, most of them not so cute and many downright destructive.

Puppies are great fun, but make sure you are prepared to take on a lot of responsibility.

If the Pug is for your child or children, be sure they clearly understand what their duties and obligations toward their pet are. And be aware that when your son discovers girls, or your daughter boys, or when other interests preoccupy them, *you* will become responsible for what you might have thought was their Pug.

Where to Get Your Pug Puppy

Now that you've determined that you can bring a Pug puppy into your life, how do you go about getting one?

Ideally, a puppy acquired from a reputable breeder is your best guarantee that you are buying a healthy, quality Pug. You may have access to such a person through a veterinarian, local kennel club or pet shop, or you may contact the Pug Dog Club of America for a list of members in your area. Of course, this is not to say that there are no reputable breeders who do not belong to the Pug Dog Club, or that you cannot find a healthy puppy through another source.

The advantages of buying from a breeder include being able to see the puppy's mother (dam) and littermates, and sometimes the father (sire) as well. The puppies should be clean, well-kept and of more or less uniform size. Often the sire himself (or a photograph of him) will be available for scrutiny. In some kennels, you may even be able to see grandparents and great-grandparents, thus giving you an accurate idea of what your puppy will look like at maturity, and what kind of temperament he will have.

Reputable breeders will also include a commitment on their part to take the puppy back at any time if you decide you cannot or do not want to keep it. Some contracts prevent you from reselling the puppy without the breeder's consent. These are normal provisions, designed for the protection of the puppy and to avoid any misunderstandings between buyer and seller. For your part, as buyer, you should ask the breeder to give you three working days to have the puppy examined by a veterinarian of your choice before the sale becomes final. This will protect you against buying an unhealthy puppy.

**PUPPY
ESSENTIALS**

Your new
puppy will
need:

food bowl

water bowl

collar

leash

I.D. tag

bed

crate

toys

grooming
supplies

Preparing for Your Puppy's Arrival

Before your puppy arrives, you should know where he will be kept in the house and what he will need.

Select a cozy corner of the house, warm and free of draughts, preferably in a busy part of the home such as the kitchen, where the puppy will quickly become used to the sights and sounds of his new home. Either a crate, a small exercise pen or a confined area should be prepared there with water and food dishes that cannot easily be overturned. In the crate or a corner, make a little nest with towels or pieces of blanket so the puppy will be cozy and comfortable.

SUPPLIES

Unless you have already done so, now is the time to visit the nearest pet supply store to purchase the things your new puppy will need. Metal water bowls and food dishes are recommended, as they are durable and dishwasher-safe. If you prefer clay bowls, be sure to buy ones made in the United States, for some imported ones are glazed with a material harmful to pets.

FOOD

The breeder should tell you what your puppy has been eating. Buy some of this food and have it on hand when your puppy arrives. Keep the puppy on the food and feeding schedule of the breeder, especially for the first few days. If you want to switch foods after that, introduce the new one slowly, gradually adding more and more to the old until it has been entirely replaced.

LEASH AND COLLAR

You will need one or two leads for walking the dog, as well as a collar or harness. If you live in a cold climate, a sweater or jacket for excursions with your Pug would be appropriate. Get a somewhat larger size than you immediately need to allow for growth.

"POOPER-SCOOPER"

You will also need a set of scoops (popularly known as pooper-scoopers) for use in your yard. Remember to take small plastic bags with you when walking your dog so you can pick up after him (something your neighbors will appreciate).

CHEW TOYS

Small-size dog biscuits are good for the teeth and also act as an amusing toy. Something to chew on becomes increasingly important as adult teeth start coming in. Do *not* buy chewing toys composed of compressed particles, as these particles disintegrate when chewed and can get stuck in the puppy's throat. Hard rubber or plastic toys are also good for chewing, as are large rawhide bones. Avoid the smaller chewsticks, as they can splinter and choke the puppy.

IDENTIFICATION

You will have to provide your puppy with some means of identification. There is always a chance that he will slip out—a visitor or meter-reader may leave the gate open, for example—and if he does, identification will maximize the chances that you will be reunited.

The first option is a common **identification tag** attached to the puppy's collar, bearing your name and phone number. This is the first thing someone who finds your Pug will look for, and the information on it is straightforward and accessible. However, puppies can easily slip out of collars, and tags can fall off, so it is important to have a more permanent method of identification as well.

A **microchip** can also be used to identify your dog. A veterinarian will inject a tiny microchip encoded with your Pug's information under his skin. Many animal shelters and vet's offices have the scanner to read the chip, and it cannot get lost or be removed. However, until the scanners (expensive pieces of equipment) are more widely available, it is preferable to choose another form of identification as well.

Puppies are irresistably cute, but they require lots of care, commitment and affection.

The third method is a **tattoo** of some identifying number (your Social Security number, your dog's AKC number) placed on the inside of your dog's hind leg. A tattoo is easily noticed and located and requires no sophisticated machinery to read. Anyone finding a lost dog with a tattoo will inform a vet or local animal shelter who will know what to do.

Puppy-Proofing

OUTSIDE

We hope your home has an enclosed yard where the puppy can run freely but cannot get out into the street. Pugs, unfortunately, have no fear of cars. Your yard should also be free of anything hazardous to your Pug, such as dead twigs or thorny bushes which can injure eyes, or small holes which could break legs. If you have a fence, it should be carefully inspected to insure there are no holes or gaps in it, and no places where a vigorous and mischievous puppy could escape by digging under.

If you do not have a fenced yard, it would be useful to provide at least an outside kennel area, for example, a four- by eight-foot chain-link enclosure, where the puppy could safely relieve himself. Failing that, the youngster should be walked outdoors on a lead several times a day, taking care at first that the lead is sufficiently tight around his neck so that he cannot slip out of it.

INSIDE

You will also need to puppy-proof your home. Curious puppies will get into everything everywhere. Even if you generally keep your Pug close to you or in his indoor or outdoor enclosure, there will be times when he wants to explore and you cannot watch him. Make sure your home has been "puppy-proofed" so you can be reasonably confident he won't do serious damage to himself or your home.

Securely stow away all household cleaners and other poisonous products such as antifreeze which, unfortunately, dogs seem to love the taste of. Keep all electrical cords out of reach and secure electrical outlets.

Make sure you have removed poisonous plants from your

Puppies are adventuresome and curious, so make sure your house and home have been thoroughly "puppy-proofed."

house and garden. Puppies, like babies, put everything into their mouths, and you need to make sure there's nothing dangerous they can get into. Inside, dangerous plants include poinsettia, ivy and philodendron. Outside, holly, hydrangea and azalea are among the plants your puppy should steer clear of. The bulbs and root systems of daffodils, tulips and others are also poisonous.

Bringing Home Your Pug Puppy

4

Few of life's pleasures can equal that of introducing a new puppy into the family. It is a delight that will be shared by the puppy himself only if you have given careful thought to the event and made detailed preparations.

A puppy should be at least eight weeks old before being separated from mother and littermates. He should be completely weaned and able to eat solid or semisolid food. If you have decided upon a puppy younger than eight weeks old, it would be wise to ask the breeder to keep him for you until he has reached that age.

When you pick your puppy up, you should receive a bill of sale of some sort, acknowledging that you have paid the agreed price, a copy of the puppy's pedigree and registration application or certificate (if he is registered with the AKC), a record of immunization shots and—hopefully—instructions and guidelines on the youngster's care and feeding.

With all the paperwork and preparations out of the way, the great moment finally arrives when the puppy is handed to you and becomes yours. Just remember that this is a completely new and overwhelming experience for your puppy. Before this, his mother and littermates have been his whole world. Try to make the experience as comforting and unthreatening as possible for him.

On the ride home, the puppy is best placed on a blanket or towel, kept warm, petted gently and spoken to in

HOUSEHOLD DANGERS

Curious puppies and inquisitive dogs get into trouble not because they are bad, but simply because they want to investigate the world around them. It's our job to protect our dogs from harmful substances, like the following:

IN THE HOUSE

cleaners, especially pine oil

perfumes, colognes, aftershaves

medications, vitamins

office and craft supplies

electric cords

chicken or turkey bones

chocolate

some house and garden plants, like ivy, oleander and poinsettia

IN THE GARAGE

antifreeze

garden supplies, like snail and slug bait, pesticides, fertilizers, mouse and rat poisons a low and soothing voice. He will probably tremble and shiver for a while before settling down. A spare towel or blanket is useful if there are any "accidents" en route. (You will soon become used to keeping paper towels, spray deodorant and some small plastic bags in the car.)

If, upon arriving home, you are greeted by eager children, they should be reminded to speak softly, gently and not to quarrel over who is the first to hold the puppy. The puppy should be carefully placed in his prepared area. It is best to postpone the visits of neighbors' children until your new Pug has settled down and gained some confidence in his new surroundings.

When the puppy is placed in his new area, leave the next move up to him. If he seems inclined to play, then by all means accommodate him. If he appears frightened, leave him alone for a while but stay close by where he can watch your activities. He will soon be emboldened to show a more active interest in his surroundings.

After his initial introduction to your home, he'll probably want to take a nap. If so, let him sleep for as long as he wishes, keeping in mind that this has all been an overwhelming experience for him.

Visiting the Veterinarian

If you have not already done so, now is the time to call and make an appointment for your veterinarian to examine the puppy. When you go, be sure to take the puppy's immunization record with you as well as any other health-related data you may have.

You should also make a point to ask your vet about heartworm and flea preventive. Ask her or him about a periodic heartworm and flea preventive, at what age it should begin, and if it is necessary to continue this treatment year-round or seasonally. Heartworm is a *major killer* of dogs, so this is very important. Also ask if you will be notified when the next series of immunizations is due, and make an appointment to have these shots administered.

Assuming your new puppy passes inspection with flying colors, the next step is to notify his breeder of this fact so that the sale to you is completely finalized. Then send in his registration papers to the AKC (if appropriate); you will receive new papers showing the change of ownership.

The First Days

For the first few days, the new puppy should be watched carefully to ensure that everything is normal. Watch especially for something resembling little grains of rice in his stool, which is a sign of tapeworm. This is not uncommon in young puppies and the vet can sometimes miss this on first examination. It requires a check by the vet.

If anything is amiss during the first few days, call the breeder to discuss the matter and, if it seems appropriate, call your vet too. If the puppy shows any signs of abnormality that cannot be readily identified, explained and corrected, this is the time to return the puppy either in exchange for another, or for a refund. If you keep a defective puppy at this point, you will be unable to take him back once you have become attached to him!

Don't be upset if your puppy walks through his food or even goes to sleep in the food dish. At this age, motor control is still not quite developed, and you may note that occasionally your pup goes backward when his intent is clearly to go forward.

ASK FOR ADVICE

During this period, your puppy's breeder and vet are your best friends. While it is all too easy to bother them with any number of little concerns, there should be no hesitation about calling either or both of them about a real problem. The puppy's breeder is probably the most knowledgeable about characteristics of the breed and common problems Pug puppy owners will encounter. If you have chosen a reputable, reliable breeder, his/her advice can be invaluable. If you know any other Pug owners in your community, they should also be very helpful.

Bringing an Adult Pug into Your Life

Bringing an adult dog into your life can be as rewarding as having a puppy, although the adjustment period may be a little longer.

If your new Pug is not a puppy, the way you treat him will be largely governed by what you can find out about his past. If he has come to you from a comfortable home where he was loved and cared for, his adjustment to your home should be quick and painless even if he has just lost a beloved master or mistress. Once in your home, he will probably select his own favorite place for naps and resting; if there is furniture he should not use, try to either keep him from the room in question

or provide some sort of barrier to discourage him from selecting it. Once he has selected his favorite place or places, he is unlikely to change his mind.

He may also select a favorite family member at first, picking the one who in his mind most closely resembles his previous master or mistress. This should not be cause for jealousy or envy on the part of other family members, as the new Pug will quite soon be friends with all.

The mature Pug who comes to you after a traumatic experience will require an exceptional degree of understanding, patience and tolerance on your part. Unfortunately, you may not be able to determine much about his past if he is a stray, an impounded dog or an accident victim. A careful examination of his body by you or your vet should reveal any signs of accident or physical abuse. At any rate, he comes to you having experienced pain, most likely at the hands of a human, and so will have a natural mistrust for humans at first. Past mental abuse is perhaps the most difficult to overcome, because you will not know its nature.

Your only recourse is to treat your new Pug with great love, tenderness and care and to observe closely and guard against any particular motion or noise that causes him to cower, withdraw or show signs of self-defense. Your efforts may have to continue for several months and may from time to time be discouraging but, with persistence, your Pug will gradually readjust to all the normal and endearing attitudes of this breed.

In accepting a "rescue" Pug, you should be aware in your own mind that you are responsible not only for feeding this dog and providing shelter, but you may also be incurring possibly expensive and continuing veterinary bills for the future. If you are not fully prepared to accept this possibility, you should not accept a "rescue" dog with an unknown background.

Feeding
Your
Pug

Because the normal, healthy Pug is firmly convinced that more of just about anything is better, we must be particularly careful about what we feed Pugsy.

Different Food for Different Stages

Just as with people, each stage of a dog's life and each change in condition requires a different diet. While it is perfectly all right to feed growing puppies up to 31 or 32 percent protein, you are asking for serious kidney problems if you give such protein-rich food to a mature dog. Similarly, what you feed a female who is bearing puppies or nursing will differ from what she is offered at other times. When a Pug reaches five or six years of age, former dietary standards no longer apply; the same food that was healthy six months ago is now unnecessary and, in all likelihood, harmful.

Generally, three different formulas are necessary for the stages of any Pug's life: (1) growth, pregnancy and heavy stress require approximately the same diet—one that's protein-rich; (2) normal periods for the mature dog call for a "maintenance" diet, in which most nutritional ingredients are reduced; and (3) old folks and couch potatoes require a drastic nutritional decrease.

Protein

The most important element in dog food is protein, but more is not necessarily better, and in fact it can be harmful in some situations. For mature dogs with average activity levels, 15 to 20 percent protein is suitable. The older and less active the dog is, the lower his protein requirements. For growing puppies, 29 percent protein is a minimum amount. Dogs in emotionally, physically or environmentally stressful situations need about 25 percent protein.

What Kind of Food?

If you shop at a supermarket, you have probably been overwhelmed by the amount and variety of dog food available. If you are perplexed, I suggest that initially you avoid the lowest priced food and stick to known brands. Cheaper brands might show the same percentage of protein, for example, but may use a quality of protein that

---

TYPES OF FOODS/TREATS

There are three types of commercially available dog food—dry, canned and semimoist—and a huge assortment of treats (lucky dogs!) to feed your dog. Which should you choose?

Dry and canned foods contain similar ingredients. The primary difference between them is their moisture content. The moisture is not just water. It's blood and broth, too, the very things that dogs adore. So while canned food is more palatable, dry food is more economical, convenient and effective in controlling tartar buildup. Most owners feed a 25% canned/75% dry diet to give their dogs the benefit of both. Just be sure your dog is getting the nutrition he needs (you and your veterinarian can determine this).

Semimoist foods have the flavor dogs love and the convenience owners want. However, they tend to contain excessive amounts of artificial colors and preservatives.

Dog treats come in every size, shape and flavor imaginable, from organic cookies shaped like postmen to beefy chew sticks. Dogs seem to love them all, so enjoy the variety. Just be sure not to overindulge your dog. Factor treats into her regular meal sizes.

your dog cannot utilize as well. If you are uncertain of the quality of food available in the large markets, your best assurance will be to use the "premium" dog food normally sold by veterinarians and large feed stores. This is what breeders exhibiting in shows and rearing top-quality dogs for competition generally use; it may cost more, but they feel it's worth it.

DRY FOOD

Dog food is available as kibble—dry food broken into manageable-sized pieces and packaged in bags. Overall, dry food is preferable, not only because it is the most economical, but also because, pound for pound, it is more nutritious. If there is a difference in kibble size, choose the smallest for your Pug (the size for Toy or small dogs). If you have only one Pug, choose the smallest available bag, first to be sure your dog will like it and, secondly, to be sure it will be consumed before it starts to get stale. Although dry food contains a preservative, it has a limited shelf life and should probably be consumed within four to six weeks. A dry food that uses vitamin E as a preservative is preferred.

TO SUPPLEMENT OR NOT TO SUPPLEMENT?

If you're feeding your dog a diet that's correct for her developmental stage and she's alert, healthy-looking and neither over- nor underweight, you don't need to add supplements. These include table scraps as well as vitamins and minerals. In fact, a growing puppy is in danger of developing musculoskeletal disorders by oversupplementation. If you have any concerns about the nutritional quality of the food you're feeding, discuss them with your veterinarian.

Dry food also helps to keep teeth clean and tartar-free, much like hard dog biscuits. If you do decide to feed your Pug canned food, mix a bit of the soft food with kibble. Otherwise you are putting your Pug at greater risk for teeth and gum problems.

CANNED FOOD

Moist or canned dog food is also available; it is good but more expensive. The protein content shown on the labels will be much lower than that shown on the dry food labels, usually between 8 and 12 percent. The canned labels also show mineral content, as a rule. If canned food is chosen, the price will range widely depending upon the ingredients used, pure beef being the most expensive.

Many owners will mix small quantities of canned or moist dog food with kibble. This improves the palatability of the dry food while still retaining the dental benefits and high nutritional content of the kibble.

A nutritionally complete, quality brand of dry food will keep adult Pugs with average activity levels in top shape.

Semimoist Food

Last, semimoist food is available, sometimes masquerading as "dog burger" or something similar. It is usually dyed red and looks very appetizing to the human eye (which is why it is dyed red). Most brands contain quite a bit of sugar and sodium. While the red color and "hamburger style" may appeal to humans, dogs don't care. High amounts of food coloring, sugar and sodium are harmful and unhealthy. If you do decide to offer this kind of food to your Pug, consider offering it as a treat rather than a staple.

How Much Should You Feed Your Pug?

How much and how often? Experts will argue endlessly that two meals daily is best for the average adult Pug.

Others feel that a single meal daily is all that is required and that a dog who is hungrier will eat better.

Pug puppies, once they are weaned, should have four meals offered daily for the first three months, reduced to three until about eight months, and finally either one or two thereafter. If your Pug does not finish his meal, reduce the number of daily servings by one.

If you are feeding dry food, many Pugs prefer that it be moistened with warm water before serving. If you feel that your dog ought to be eating more, try adding a couple of tablespoons moist food to the moistened dry food. If he still doesn't eat well and is losing weight, consult your veterinarian.

Water

Always, always have fresh water available for your Pug.

Treats

While avoiding table scraps or leftovers, there is nothing wrong with an occasional treat. Good-quality dog biscuits have about the same nutritional value as an equal amount of kibble and, in addition, help to reduce tartar on the teeth. Another small but tasty treat is small bits of semimoist food. These should be considered more as rewards than as food, but don't forget to figure them into your dog's daily calorie intake.

Don'ts

For the most part, your Pug will not receive a balanced diet if he is fed from the table or given leftovers. Feeding from the table will also encourage the habit of

---

HOW MANY MEALS A DAY?

Individual dogs vary in how much they should eat to maintain a desired body weight—not too fat, but not too thin. Puppies need several meals a day, while older dogs may need only one. Determine how much food keeps your adult dog looking and feeling her best. Then decide how many meals you want to feed with that amount. Like us, most dogs love to eat, and offering two meals a day is more enjoyable for them. If you're worried about overfeeding, make sure you measure correctly and abstain from adding tidbits to the meals.

Whether you feed one or two meals, only leave your dog's food out for the amount of time it takes her to eat it—10 minutes, for example. Freefeeding (when food is available any time) and leisurely meals encourage picky eating. Don't worry if your dog doesn't finish all her dinner in the allotted time. She'll learn she should.

begging, which will detract from your own pleasure at the table and could be a major embarrassment if guests are present.

Most forms of candy or highly spiced or seasoned foods will upset your Pug's nutritional balance. Special mention must be made of chocolate, which contains an ingredient poisonous to dogs and can even be fatal.

A Pug who's well-fed and fit has no trouble with agility tricks like this one.

Supplementation

Some pharmaceutical companies are producing dog vitamins. Are they necessary? Examine the label on the dog food you have chosen, and you will note that it already contains vitamins in amounts determined by veterinary dietitians. Adding vitamins to such food would unbalance it and could possibly be dangerous to your Pug's health. If, on the other hand, your veterinarian determines that your Pug needs additional vitamins, then by all means follow his or her advice.

MORE MINERALS MAY BE HARMFUL

Kidney failure is a major cause of canine deaths. It is usually the end result of a prolonged period of progressively damaged kidneys caused directly or indirectly by excessive intake of protein, phosphorus, calcium and/or sodium.

To avoid such a progression toward kidney failure, diets should be limited to the minimum percentages of such ingredients to the extent possible, and adjusted to the individual situation of each dog for each period of his life.

Using high-quality commercial dog food labeled "complete and balanced" is more likely to achieve desired results than mixing your own or feeding scraps and leftovers.

An excess of calcium, found in a number of pet foods, reduces phosphorus, iron, zinc and copper absorption, thus risking a deficiency in these minerals. Zinc deficiency, especially in puppies, can lead to skin sores, shrinking testicles (in males), slow healing, lowered immunity and a number of other problems. Even if excess calcium is not enough to cause a detectable problem, it will tend to slow growth.

A dog's requirement for sodium is very low. Some popular brands of dry dog food are believed to contain approximately twenty times more than the average dog requires. A dog's reaction to excessive sodium is similar to that of humans, leading to hypertension which, in turn, may develop into heart disease, hardening of the arteries, or kidney disease.

Unfortunately, manufacturers are not required to reveal the mineral content of their product, and some do not. This information can be obtained from the manufacturer, often by calling an 800 number on the food's wrapper.

HOW TO READ THE DOG FOOD LABEL

With so many choices on the market, how can you be sure you are feeding the right food for your dog? The information is all there on the label—if you know what you're looking for.

Look for the nutritional claim right up top. Is the food "100% nutritionally complete"? If so, it's for nearly all life stages; "growth and maintenance," on the other hand, is for early development; puppy foods are marked as such, as are foods for senior dogs.

Ingredients are listed in descending order by weight. The first three or four ingredients will tell you the bulk of what the food contains. Look for the highest-quality ingredients, like meats and grains, to be among them.

The Guaranteed Analysis tells you what levels of protein, fat, fiber and moisture are in the food, in that order. While these numbers are meaningful, they won't tell you much about the quality of the food. Nutritional value is in the dry matter, not the moisture content.

In many ways, seeing is believing. If your dog has bright eyes, a shiny coat, a good appetite and a good energy level, chances are his diet's fine. Your dog's breeder and your veterinarian are good sources of advice if you're still confused.

When using a complete and balanced commercial dog food, do not add supplements unless advised to do so by your veterinarian. If you are confused about your Pug's diet, your vet can offer you advice, or you can contact other Pug owners and breeders through the Pug Dog Club (address on page 33).

chapter 6

Grooming
Your
Pug

Pugs are short-coated and naturally clean little dogs. The Pug owner doesn't have to worry about huge grooming expenses. Unfortunately, some Pug owners seem to think this means little or no care is needed. True, compared with a Poodle or Yorkshire Terrier, little coat care is required. But there are a number of things the Pug owner must do to keep his or her Pug healthy, comfortable and happy.

Coat Care

Let us take a look at the Pug's coat. It should be quite short and have a sheen or glisten to it. It should not shed excessively. A Pug's coat is a good barometer of his overall condition. While a daily brushing should take care of normal shedding, excessive shedding might mean that the dog has some sort of problem, for the coat is one of the first things affected when a dog begins to have a health problem. If your Pug has been stressed in some manner—a lengthy car ride, an attack by another dog or even a significant change of weather—extra shedding can be expected. If the excessive shedding does not lessen after brushing or stripping, it is a good idea to have your Pug examined by a veterinarian.

Have a grooming table or other nonslip surface available on which to groom your Pug.

SHEDDING

So now you know it. Pugs shed. Some books say they don't, but they do. This is true more for the double-coated fawns than for the blacks, but all Pugs shed. Some may do it seasonally, some fairly steadily. When they are shedding, the fawn owner is advised not to wear dark clothing, and the owner of a black Pug should not wear light-colored clothing. A Pug's hair tends to cling to clothing and requires a good, stiff clothes brush or some sort of sticky device to remove it.

If the shedding is heavy, one should use a slicker brush (available at most pet stores). This brush has fine steel teeth mounted in a rubber base, and is quite efficient in removing loose hair.

BRUSHING

The effects of shedding are minimized by taking a few minutes each day to brush the coat with an ordinary bristle (not nylon) hairbrush to remove loose hair and stimulate the follicles to produce the natural oils that give the coat its sheen. If your Pug is not accustomed to this daily routine, he will fidget and fuss a bit. With repetition, a few sharp commands and sufficient encouragement, he will soon get used to the brushing and, in fact, will look forward to it.

You will probably want to have a small table or cabinet top to place the dog on while brushing him, covered with a bath mat to keep him from slipping. After you have finished his daily brushing, and while he is still on the table, a careful study of his coat will reveal any sores or "hot spots."

While inspecting the coat, be alert for any signs of flea or tick infestation. Ticks are big enough to be easily seen, especially if they are engorged. They are disease carriers and should be plucked off at once with a pair of tweezers or a hemostat. Fleas are harder to spot, but they usually leave a telltale clue behind in the form of tiny black specks of feces, known more politely as "flea dirt." The most likely place to find it is on the skin at the base of the spine, just forward of the tail.

Nose

Next, examine your Pug's head. Start by placing your thumb between his eyes just above his nose fold and push the skin back so that the entire top of the nose can be seen. Food will sometimes become lodged under the nose fold. As this area is usually moist, sores may develop there. Gently clean under the nose fold with a cotton ball or a piece of old toweling, and then rub a small quantity of petroleum jelly on the skin and nose.

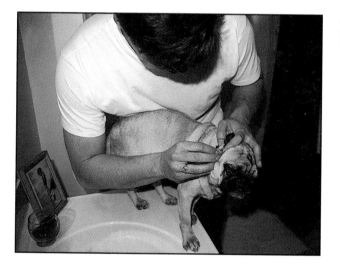

Ears should be cleaned regularly and carefully.

Ears

Check each ear, holding the flap upright. Gently insert a cotton swab (not very far) and clean out any accumulated matter lodged there. Use a different end of the swab for each ear. If there is a dark brown, putrid-smelling substance, your pug probably has an ear infection and needs to be seen by a veterinarian.

Eyes

From there, inspect the eyes. As Pugs are prone to eye injury, from minor scratches to more serious puncture wounds, care should be taken to detect excessive tearing or staining under the eye, and to see if the eye color has changed. An eye wound will usually look light blue. If this discoloration is noted, get your Pug to the veterinarian immediately; haste is important!

Mouth

Before leaving the head area, push back his lips far enough to inspect the teeth down to the gums. If tartar accumulation is evident or if gums are either bleeding or very pale, once again a trip to the vet's office is called for. While this and the problems mentioned above are rare and, indeed, may never occur in your Pug, it is nevertheless important that this inspection be routine.

When you give your Pug a bath, it's a good idea to use an antiflea shampoo even if you don't notice an infestation of these pests.

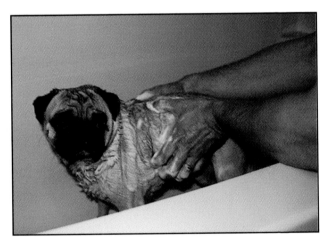

This check-up, done in any order you prefer, should assure you that Pugsy is in good health, or will alert you to any problem requiring special attention.

Bath

A dog's first bath is likely to be a bit of a contest of wills, particularly with a young puppy. In time, he will come to enjoy all the attention that goes with bathing and will look forward to it. The Pug is a naturally clean little dog and a bath about once a month should suffice, unless, of course, he has gotten into something that should be cleaned up immediately.

SHAMPOO

The bath products sold by your vet are usually quite good, as are those found in pet stores. Some owners have reported good results from the dog shampoos found at the supermarket. Even if there is no sign of a flea or tick infestation, it is advisable to use a shampoo with antiflea/tick medication. Check to see if it contains pyrethrins; this antiflea ingredient is believed to be the safest. Most of these shampoos require the suds to remain on the dog for five to ten minutes before thoroughly rinsing. Above all, do *not* use soap or shampoo meant for humans. It is not suited for the particular conditions of a dog's coat.

A laundry tub is the best place for a bath, as you will likely have some mopping up to do afterward. Buy a removable hose with a spray head and attach it to the tub faucet. Before placing Pugsy in the tub, put a drop of mineral oil in each of his eyes so that if shampoo gets into an eye, it won't sting. After placing him in the tub, check the water's temperature before wetting him down; it should be warm but not hot. Wet his coat thoroughly before applying the shampoo, then follow the directions on the bottle. Be prepared to get a good soaking yourself if or when Pugsy decides to shake, as he probably will unless you keep a hand on him at all times.

Start to lather around the neck and head, being careful to avoid the eyes, then work down the body, legs and tail, being sure to reach all the "tight" places like under the legs, around the testicles and anal area and the base of the tail. Then rinse thoroughly, until the rinse water is clear.

DRYING

Before removing him from the tub, let him drip for a minute and squeeze as much moisture as you can from the coat. Then on he goes to the grooming table for a good toweling. This is the best part as far as he is concerned. Most Pugs love to be toweled, the rougher the better. But, again, be on guard for a good shake! This is a good time to examine his nails to see if they need clipping.

A well-groomed Pug looks healthy and clean.

If the weather is good or the house warm, and if you have toweled him thoroughly, it will do no harm to leave him loose in the laundry room or outside until he is completely dry. Otherwise, dry him with a hair dryer while he is on the grooming table. It is not necessary to get him bone dry. After that, you will probably want to clean up the bath area and clean the Pug hair from the drain strainer. In fact, you may have to clean the drain screen one or more times while you are shampooing him.

If you don't have a laundry tub, the bathtub will do. If you use the bathtub, a nonslip pad of some sort will be necessary, and be sure there is a screen over the drain to catch hair. Washing in the bathtub can be a backbreaker, however. A bath and rinse outdoors with a metal tub and garden hose can do an adequate job, but you will find that control is, at best, difficult.

While bathing will wash away much of the dog's loose coat, it will also leave a lot of it still in place. After the bath is a good time to use a slicker brush, as the excess hair will be loose and will brush out easily. If possible, this brushing is best done outdoors.

Clipping Toenails

Now we come to the potentially most difficult part of being a Pug owner: keeping the toenails short. Seldom does one encounter a Pug who will willingly allow his nails to be clipped. Often, your Pug seems sincerely convinced that you are going to inflict excruciating pain on him, causing him to resort to every acrobatic trick he knows, even to holding his breath. The easy way to avoid all this is to take him to your vet or a professional groomer and let them do it—after you leave!

For the strong of will, however, it can become a manageable procedure. There are two ways to approach it. The first is by using a grinder (available at pet stores) and an assistant. The Pug must be held firmly, while each of his sixteen nails are ground down. (The dewclaws, roughly the same as a human's thumb-nail, are usually removed from the front feet by the breeder, while Pugs' rear feet seldom have dewclaws. If your Pug still has dewclaws, those nails, too, must be shortened.)

The second method, which gets it over with faster, is to use a nail clipper (again, found at pet stores). In this method, an assistant is even more important. Have the assistant hold the Pug wrapped in a towel, while the owner does the clipping. If your Pug has white nails, the quick (or vein) in each nail can be seen, and the nail should be cut just beyond the quick. The quick will bleed if cut, so make sure you have styptic powder on hand to stop the bleeding. If your Pug has black nails, the quick cannot be seen and your judgment is your only guide. The best way to

GROOMING TOOLS

pin brush

slicker brush

flea comb

towel

mat rake

grooming glove

scissors

nail clippers

tooth-cleaning equipment

shampoo

conditioner

clippers

avoid bleeding is to clip the nails often so that the quick recedes naturally and, if the nails are kept short, you won't have a problem.

What if you don't trim the nails? As they lengthen, they will cause the dog's foot to splay out which is not only ugly but, in time, can be crippling. Long nails can also be dangerous to eyes and skin when the dog scratches himself. The nail-cutting procedure—about every two to three weeks—is a definite must.

You will have observed that we have mentioned towels a number of times in connection with bathing, nail cutting and lining your Pug's crate. A rule of thumb is: Never throw away an old towel.

Anal Glands

In discussing dog care, it is sometimes difficult to keep the conversation on a dinner table level. All dogs, including Pugs, have anal glands or sacs, located on either side of the anus. These sacs secrete a thick liquid substance with an unpleasant odor. In small dogs particularly, these glands will occasionally become impacted, causing the dog some discomfort and inducing him to drag his hindquarters on the ground or try to lick that area. This is a sign that the sacs need to be emptied, a simple but not exactly pleasant procedure. Your veterinarian can do this for you, but if you wish to save yourself a trip and a fee, you can do it yourself.

First, raise the dog's tail with one hand and hold a paper towel or tissue in the other. With the tissue hand, place your thumb and forefinger on either side of the anus, press in and squeeze gently. The secretion should be expelled into the tissue, after which the area may be gently wiped clean. Impacted anal glands can become infected and require veterinarian attention. If the discharge appears bloody or pus-like, it will be painful to the dog and will tell you that an infection is present.

This procedure is quite simple but may require some practice. If you choose to have it done by your vet, ask your vet to show you how so you can do it yourself in the future.

If consistently applied, these simple grooming procedures will keep your Pug in top shape.

Keeping Your
Pug
Healthy

The easiest way to keep your Pug healthy is to provide good preventive care and a healthy lifestyle. A complete series of vaccinations, heartworm preventive, and a one-time spaying or neutering procedure will give your Pug a healthy start and keep him free of some of the most dangerous canine conditions. By providing your Pug with daily grooming, good dental care, a nutritious diet and plenty of exercise, you are giving him the best assurance of a long and healthy life.

Once you have mastered the daily needs of your new Pug, your next step should be to locate a veterinarian who can take good care of your Pug's medical needs. Your vet should be a person in whom you have faith, who will give your new Pug the best possible care.

Choosing a Veterinarian

At your first visit, try to find out what you can about the vet and his or her experience with Pugs. Ask about other clients who own Pugs, and later contact a few of these to seek their opinion of the vet. Ask about after-hours emergency services. Is the office open on Sunday? Are X-ray and ultrasound equipment available?

Pugs, like other short-faced breeds, have their own peculiar problems, and your vet should be familiar with these. It may seem like a bother to look into all these things but, when the vet's expertise is needed, you will be glad you took the trouble.

Vaccinations

Give your vet all the immunization and health data you have on your Pug so far, then arrange a schedule for vaccinations and booster shots. Most veterinary clinics will send their clients postcard reminders when booster shots are due.

Your puppy's immunizations should be a series of shots over a period of ten to twelve weeks, and should include DHLP, parvovirus and rabies. A blood sample to ensure that your puppy is free of heartworm should be made at this time, and the vet will probably prescribe a pill to be administered each month as a preventive. The vet, of course, will keep a record of these treatments, though you may want to ask for a copy for your own records.

Puppies are more susceptible to many diseases than adult dogs, so make sure you stick to the vaccination schedule.

What Are All Those Immunizations For?

One of the first shots your Pug will receive is commonly known as DHLP. This is a cocktail mixture of several immunizations—for distemper, hepatitis, leptospirosis and parainfluenza. The vaccines themselves are very effective and seldom cause any problem except for an occasional allergic reaction (see the section on allergies).

DISTEMPER

Canine distemper at one time ravaged entire kennels. Modern vaccines are responsible for the decline of this viral disease, but cases still surface occasionally. The virus is transmitted by an infected dog's breath or other body secretions. It takes about two weeks from the time of exposure until the first signs of sickness occur. During this period, the dog's temperature may rise somewhat but will quickly return to normal. It then goes into the second phase, when the dog becomes really ill. At this stage an infected dog will pass loose and sometimes bloody stools, accompanied by vomiting. A thick discharge often closes the eyes, and depression sets in. Lack of appetite leads to weight loss and dehydration. Spasms of the head and legs may accompany the other symptoms. If your vet can bring this disease under control, all may go well for periods of up to several weeks, only to be followed by another severe attack. The virus invades the brain's nerve cells so that, even after recovery, the victim may never regain full control of his body. The best defense is to be sure your Pug's immunizations are boosted at least annually.

YOUR PUPPY'S VACCINES

Vaccines are given to prevent your dog from getting an infectious disease like canine distemper or rabies. Vaccines are the ultimate preventive medicine: they're given before your dog ever gets the disease so as to protect him from the disease. That's why it is necessary for your dog to be vaccinated routinely. Puppy vaccines start at eight weeks of age for the five-in-one DHLPP vaccine and are given every three to four weeks until the puppy is sixteen months old. Your veterinarian will put your puppy on a proper schedule and will remind you when to bring in your dog for shots.

Canine Hepatitis

Canine hepatitis is a viral disease passed from an affected dog through urine, feces or saliva. A newly infected dog will develop reddened eyes, and a discharge from the nose, mouth and eyes, accompanied by a fever. He will soon stop eating and, in severe cases, may lapse into a coma. Within six to ten days, the dog will either die or quickly recover. Immunization against hepatitis is a must.

Leptospirosis

Leptospirosis, unlike distemper and hepatitis, is a bacterial disease and is thus more curable by medication. It has become quite unusual and, in fact, a number of practicing veterinarians have never been presented with a case. A dog may pick this up through infected urine, and will soon lose his appetite and become depressed. He may show abdominal pain, develop ulcers in his mouth and on his tongue, and a yellowish eye. This is accompanied by diarrhea, often bloody, and vomiting. Damage to the digestive tract, liver and kidneys will make for a slow recovery. Even after recovery, a cured dog's illness may still be passed to other dogs through his urine. Immunization is necessary even though the disease is becoming rare.

Kennel Cough

Kennel cough, or bordatella, is normally no more serious than so-called "flu" is to people. It is, however, highly infectious and can quickly run through an entire kennel unless the patient is isolated. Symptoms are a dry, hacking cough, sometimes accompanied by a runny nose. While it will usually run its course in adult Pugs and is not known to be fatal, small dogs (including Pugs) and young puppies who are affected do need some special care, and should be kept warm in a moist atmosphere.

As kennel cough is a mix of several viruses and at least one bacterium, it can be attacked with antibiotics prescribed by your vet. Vaccines are available as part of your prevention program, and are recommended. However, as with flu, the viruses tend to mutate from season to season, so it is difficult to find a vaccine that will be effective across the board.

RABIES

Vaccination against rabies is absolutely essential and, as far as we know, is compulsory in every state. Some states require a booster annually, others every three years. Rabies is a virus transmitted to dogs by the saliva of infected dogs, foxes, raccoons, skunks and bats and possibly other woodland denizens. It is readily transmittable to humans, who then require a series of painful serum shots. There is no known cure for dogs, and the end result is death.

Symptoms may begin with some sort of behavioral change; a shy dog may become aggressive, or a lively, outgoing one appear to be shy. The dog will be increasingly unresponsive, will resent being handled, and may develop diarrhea and begin to vomit. Eventually, he collapses, becomes comatose and dies. It is a dreadful disease and every pet owner should take all possible measures to shield his dog from exposure. Should you see a wild animal acting strangely or an unknown dog exhibiting some of the symptoms, call your wildlife or humane officer immediately.

Unfortunately, we have not ex-hausted the list of diseases to which your Pug could easily succumb, and two in particular deserve mention: they are parvovirus ("parvo") and coronavirus. These viral diseases were unknown as recently as 1978, when they broke out in several large kennels in the United States with

---

WHEN TO CALL THE VET

In any emergency situation, you should call your veterinarian immediately. You can make the difference in your dog's life by staying as calm as possible when you call and by giving the doctor or the assistant as much information as possible before you leave for the clinic. That way, the vet will be able to take immediate, specific action to remedy your dog's situation.

Emergencies include acute abdominal pain, suspected poisoning, snakebite, burns, frostbite, shock, dehydration, abnormal vomiting or bleeding, and deep wounds. You are the best judge of your dog's health, as you live with and observe him every day. Don't hesitate to call your veterinarian if you suspect trouble.

disastrous results and the loss of many dogs. Veterinary schools and pharmaceutical manufacturers across the country immediately set their research staffs to work to isolate the virus and to develop a vaccine to deal with it. Particular mention should be made of the efforts of Cornell University in this respect. These diseases have now spread to every corner of the globe, but, happily, effective vaccines are now available.

Parvovirus

Parvovirus is transmitted primarily through the feces of an infected dog. It is readily transported on the hair or feet of a dog, or can be brought into anyone's home on shoes, contaminated crates, or any other object. Even apparently healthy dogs with a mild infection can spread the contagion if brought into contact with other dogs.

Dogs with "parvo" often will stop eating and act depressed as much as twenty-four hours before other symptoms occur. Vomiting follows, then diarrhea, which will probably become bloody. They will have a high fever, over 105 degrees in puppies. Some dogs may be mildly affected, while others, in spite of a vet's best efforts, may die. Young dogs are the most susceptible, particularly under three months of age, although the disease can be fatal at any age. There is no effective treatment.

Immunizations are available which have a high percentage of effectiveness against both parvovirus and coronavirus, a similar viral infection. As puppies "inherit" a certain immunity from their mother, care must be taken not to administer this vaccine too early, as the mother's immunity in the puppies will nullify it.

As noted, the several diseases which have been described have symptoms in common, although each requires its own unique treatment. It is therefore important that you not assume that any of these symptoms will simply go away. Let your veterinarian make that decision. The few dollars this will cost may save your Pug's life!

Internal Parasites

Sooner or later, it is close to inevitable that your Pug is going to pick up some kind of worms, so the responsible pet owner should be aware of the most likely ones, and what the symptoms are.

HEARTWORM

By far the most important is heartworm. Until a few decades ago, heartworm was quite rare in the United States, but in the late 1960s and 1970s, it began to spread rapidly throughout the southern states. Today, it is found in all states, except possibly Hawaii. It is preventable, it is treatable, but, if not prevented or treated, it is fatal.

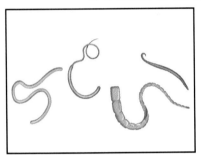

Common internal parasites (l-r): roundworm, whipworm, tapeworm and hookworm.

Heartworms, as the name implies, live inside a dog's heart and the adjacent major blood vessels. The disease is transmitted through mosquitoes. Once in residence, heartworms will reproduce, and the resultant larvae (microfilariae) will circulate throughout the dog's bloodstream. Along comes a mosquito, bites the dog and ingests its blood, larvae and all. After a short period, the mosquito bites another dog and, in the process, deposits heartworm larvae in the second dog. The larvae then develops and, in time, enters the dog's heart as a fully mature worm. In time, they clog the dog's heart to the point where the heart function becomes impaired and eventually the dog dies.

Once your Pug is about a year old, your vet will be able to detect such an invasion by analyzing a blood sample. Prior to this, the larvae will not be sufficiently developed to be detectable. Most cases occur in dogs at about middle age. If it turns out that your dog has heartworm, it can be treated, usually with an arsenic-based compound. Arsenic will kill the heartworm, but it also acts as a poison on your dog as well. Another danger is that the killed heartworms will clog up the circulatory system. Symptoms that indicate the possibility of heartworm infestation are shortness of breath, shallow coughing and easily tiring. If such symptoms are observed, head straight for the vet's office.

Obviously, prevention is the *only* desirable course. Tablets administered monthly or daily are available from your vet. It is most important that it be given to Pugsy regularly on the same day of each month. Before starting Pugsy on a heartworm prevention medication, your vet must determine that no heartworms are present. The safest course is to begin the monthly treatment before your Pug is six months old, prior to the time when heartworms could mature. Then, at six-month intervals, he should be checked, especially if you have missed a dosage.

HOOKWORM

Hookworms have a life cycle of fourteen days, spent inside the dog's intestine. In the first week, the larvae develop and begin to reach and attach to the dog's intestinal wall. They begin to feed on the intestinal tissue, changing feeding sites as many as six times a day. Hookworm damage leads to severe blood loss, anemia and intestinal damage. They also risk making the dog more vulnerable to intestinal diseases.

While treatment to eliminate hookworm is inexpensive, it is not totally effective. It is therefore wise to have your vet do a fecal check for hookworm on a monthly basis. Pug puppies, because of their small size, are particularly susceptible to hookworm damage and should ideally be checked about every other week until they are three months old.

ROUNDWORM

Roundworms are extremely common, especially in puppies, and can be fatal to young Pugs if not controlled. Dogs will ingest roundworm eggs from the soil, particularly if their outdoor exercise area is limited. These eggs hatch into tiny worms that pass from the dog's intestines to the liver and lungs, and then back to the intestines, where they mature. Infected female dogs can pass the roundworms on to their puppies both before they are born or while they are nursing. At a minimum, roundworm will depress a puppy's health, cause diarrhea, and give the puppy's belly a distended appearance.

Give your pets as much space as possible outside, keeping their environment as clean as possible and free of fecal matter, both inside and out. While your vet is checking for hookworm, he should also check for roundworm.

WHIPWORM

In some aspects, whipworm is similar to roundworm. Dogs will swallow the eggs from the soil, especially if the dogs are confined to a small outdoor area. Roundworms also lodge in the dog's intestines and can severely irritate the intestinal lining, causing weight loss and considerable discomfort. Detection of whipworm through stool examination is sometimes difficult, and it may be necessary to examine several stools over a period of days before they are detected. Also, it is sometimes necessary to repeat the treatment several times in order to eliminate the infestation completely.

TAPEWORM

Tapeworm is common but many veterinarians consider it to be relatively harmless, and eliminating it largely a cosmetic matter. Tapeworms can be detected in a dog's stool, appearing as small white grains about the size of rice. They are transmitted from one dog to another by fleas, so that if you have more than one dog, the others should be treated as well. Your vet can prescribe an effective medication to eliminate these pests.

GIARDIA

This parasite is actually a protozoan that gets into your Pug's system through infected drinking water. Giardia invades the intestinal tract and the primary symptom is diarrhea. Puppies may be particularly susceptible. These parasites are common to wild animals in many areas, so if you have been out walking with your Pug in a wild area and he develops diarrhea, suspect giardia. Make sure to see your veterinarian for diagnosis and treatment.

If you plan to be out hiking with your Pug, bring along drinking water for him as well as for yourself. Avoid unsanitary places where lots of dogs congregate. These sites are breeding grounds for all kinds of pests.

External Parasites

FLEAS

Let us turn to perhaps the most stubborn and bothersome of the external parasites—fleas. There is no part of the United States that is entirely free of fleas, and a number of the southern states are plagued by them year-round. The hot, dry months, usually August and September, produce the most favorable climate for the emergence of adult fleas. An adult flea can live for as long as two years, but can reproduce only if it feeds on blood. For that reason, the most likely areas for reproduction and habitation are spots where a dog will spend much of its time. When the flea bites your dog, it not only causes irritation but can also infect your dog with tapeworm.

Although adult fleas are large enough to be seen with the naked eye as tiny black specks, you are more likely to find their "leavings" on your dog rather than the fleas themselves. If you observe tiny black spots on your Pug's skin, it is probably flea feces. Dogs infested with

---

FIGHTING FLEAS

Remember, the fleas you see on your dog are only part of the problem—the smallest part! To rid your dog and home of fleas, you need to treat your dog *and* your home. Here's how:

• Identify where your pet(s) sleep. These are "hot spots."

• Clean your pets' bedding regularly by vacuuming and washing.

• Spray "hot spots" with a non-toxic, long-lasting flea larvicide.

• Treat outdoor "hot spots" with insecticide.

• Kill eggs on pets with a product containing insect growth regulators (IGRs).

• Kill fleas on pets per your veterinarian's recommendation.

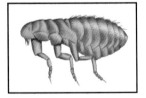
fleas will bite and scratch themselves often, which can roughen the skin to the point where it is vulnerable to secondary bacterial infection. Repeated flea bites will sensitize your pet to the point where a single flea can cause a serious allergic reaction.

To effectively eliminate fleas, both your dog and premises must be treated.

Especially in warm climates, it seems to be all but impossible to be completely free of fleas, and the most you can hope for is to keep the pests at bay. To do this requires that both your pet and your premises be treated. Ridding your dog of fleas by itself will not be effective, as he will immediately become reinfested from his untreated environment. Use a flea shampoo when you bathe your Pug, and treat him with a flea powder or spray approximately every ten days. This should be done outdoors or over newspaper, as fleas will fall off the dog during treatment and reinfest the area unless they can be immediately disposed of. To maximize your efforts, treat the premises at the same time the dog is treated.

If your home is treated periodically by an exterminator, be sure to advise the exterminator to include a flea insecticide in whatever solution he uses, paying particular attention to areas where your Pug normally spends his time. Alternatively, you may purchase aerosol flea insecticides and do the job yourself, concentrating on dog bedding, cracks in floors, around baseboards and beneath carpets. Treatment should be repeated in ten to fourteen days to eliminate newly-hatched fleas. In extreme cases, it may be necessary to "bomb" the house by setting off several insecticide "bombs." Before activating the "bombs," you and all pets should be prepared to evacuate the building for at least two hours.

The flea is a die-hard pest.

Once your Pug has been freed of fleas, he should be given a pill monthly (furnished by your vet) which will kill flea eggs and thus prevent their hatching out.

TICKS

Another common pest is the brown dog tick. This tick can live for up to two hundred days without attaching to a dog. Once they are engorged with a dog's blood, they will drop off the animal and lay between one thousand and

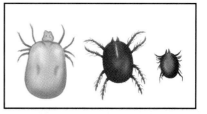

three thousand eggs. In the house, the eggs are usually found along baseboards, window and door casings, curtains, furniture, and around the edges of rugs. Between feeding, the ticks themselves usually hide in the same areas as their eggs.

Three types of ticks (l-r): the wood tick, brown dog tick and deer tick.

Less common but still pesky are American dog ticks, usually found outdoors along paths and trails and in grass and low shrubbery. These ticks will grasp on to any passing dog and immediately start their meal. When feeding, they attach two "claws" to the dog's skin and then insert a barbed mouthpiece through the skin through which blood is sucked. Because of the nature of their mouthpieces, they are not easily removed.

The American dog tick may carry Rocky Mountain spotted fever, tularemia and other diseases that will affect humans but not dogs. Take extra care when removing a tick from your dog, as you could possibly be exposed to any number of diseases.

Use tweezers to remove ticks from your dog.

Once observed, the tick should be removed at once. Swab it with alcohol or nail polish remover to encourage it to loosen its grip. Then remove it with tweezers, making sure the headpiece has been removed as well. Disinfect the bite, and monitor the bite area for the next few days to make sure it doesn't become infected.

A tick infestation calls for action and, if the infestation is heavy, it will be necessary to cleanse your Pug, your house and the outdoor areas frequented by the dog. Sevin or malathion dust may be rubbed into the Pug's skin, being careful to avoid the eyes, nose and mouth. In severe cases, a dip similar to a flea dip is called for. Insecticide should be applied inside the house to those areas where ticks are likely to hide (see above), with special attention to areas where your Pug spends most of his time. Outside the house, the same chemicals used inside may be used in suspected areas. Clear brush or low bushes in frequented areas and burn the resulting garden trash.

Although pesticides, if properly used, should not affect your dogs, great care should be taken to keep them away from dog food and water. Ingestion could be fatal.

Spaying and Neutering

There are a number of reasons people consider having puppies: Having puppies is a natural thing and is "good" for the dog, having a nice litter is an easy way to "make a little money on the side," and having a litter would be an educational experience for the children.

Having puppies is a natural thing, of course, but it is not necessarily good for your female Pug. In fact, carrying a litter to term, whelping the pups, then suckling them for five or six weeks places a very heavy burden on your female Pug. The very act of whelping usually is a very painful and exhausting experience. The result could be either no puppies, just one (usually over-sized) puppy, or one or more pups either born dead or who survive for just a few days. The list of things that could go wrong during the first three weeks after birth is lengthy indeed, and you may be called upon to decide between life and death for a sickly puppy.

But let's say things go reasonably well. In that case, the owner must plan to devote at least three full days and sleepless nights to caring for mother and puppies, seeing that they all get nursed and monitoring the mother's health. You will need someone to help you with the whelping, hopefully someone who has experience with small, flat-faced dogs. The whole process can be emotionally draining and physically exhausting.

A spayed female will avoid the pain and the risk of bearing puppies and will probably retain both her youthful vigor and appearance longer than otherwise. In addition, she will not be at risk for pyometra, a life-threatening uterine infection, and will be at decreased risk for mammary tumors.

Is breeding good for your male Pug? In fact, it is neither good nor bad for him, but once he has been used in breeding, his house manners are likely to be forgotten as he "marks his territory" following his newly-found masculinity. If he lives with another dog, he is likely to become more aggressive and "territorially-minded." A neutered male will, if anything, be happier, less stressed and generally gentler and friendlier, and will also be free of testicular cancer and other diseases of the reproductive system.

As far as making a little extra money, breeding is not an easy way to do it. When one factors in all the expenses incurred—numerous veterinary visits, special food, medication, and the countless hours you spend stressed and sleepless, it's clear that breeding is in fact an expensive hobby. An attempt to earn a

---

ADVANTAGES OF SPAY/NEUTER

The greatest advantage of spaying (for females) or neutering (for males) your dog is that you are guaranteed your dog will not produce puppies. There are too many puppies already available for too few homes. There are other advantages as well.

ADVANTAGES OF SPAYING

No messy heats.

No "suitors" howling at your windows or waiting in your yard.

Decreased incidences of pyometra (disease of the uterus) and breast cancer.

ADVANTAGES OF NEUTERING

Lessens male aggressive and territorial behaviors, but doesn't affect the dog's personality. Behaviors are often owner-induced, so neutering is not the only answer, but it is a good start.

Prevents the need to roam in search of bitches in season.

Decreased incidences of urogenital diseases.

bit extra by breeding will likely lead to disappointment and financial loss.

As concerns breeding for the purpose of educating children, it is often the case that the observing children are not only educated but also traumatized if either the mother or one or more puppies dies in the process—an event not at all out of the ordinary.

We can recall all too clearly the anticipation as our granddaughter looked forward to having a litter of puppies in the house. A "nursery" had been prepared, a box with a heating pad to hold the newborns. After several hours of labor pains, it became obvious that the expectant mother Pug was having difficulties and had to be taken to the veterinary hospital for some professional attention. With her went the heated box for the expected puppies. The affair ended with the vet having to perform a cesarean section; none of the five puppies survived. We arrived home with an exhausted Pug and an empty puppy box. As we opened the door, our granddaughter eagerly greeted us and, of course, wanted to see the puppies right away. What she saw was the empty box. That young lady is now grown, married and the mother of two—but recalling that incident still brings tears to her eyes.

Administering Medication

TO GIVE A PILL

The easiest way to do this is to wrap the pill in a soft tasty snack—like cheese. Offer the dog a pill-less bite of the treat first, and then offer him the bit with the medicine in it. He should polish it off, pill and all without a problem, but watch him for a few moments after he appears to have swallowed to make sure the pill went with the treat.

If he manages to extract the pill from the food and keeps spitting it out, open his jaws wide and tilt his head back. Drop the pill into the back of his throat and massage the outside of the throat until you see him swallow. Again, make sure the pill is gone!

LIQUID MEDICATION

The easiest way to give liquid medication is with an oral syringe or turkey baster. Fill the syringe with the correct amount of medication, and tilt the dog's head slightly back. Squeeze the medication between the cheek and the molars, forming a little pocket with the skin of the cheek. This way you'll be sure he doesn't inhale the liquid and choke.

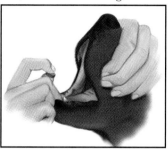

To give a pill, open the mouth wide, then drop it in the back of the throat.

OINTMENT

To apply eye ointment, pull the lower lid out and squeeze the correct amount of medication into the pocket formed by the lower lid. When the dog blinks, the ointment will be distributed around the eye.

Applying skin ointment is very simple; just spread the dog's fur and apply the ointment directly to the skin as best you can. If the area is infected or raw, be extra gentle and careful.

Applying the ointment may be simple, but the real challenge is making sure it stays on your Pug. His first instinct will probably be to lick it off, further irritating the wound and eliminating any benefits of the medication. To prevent this, your vet may suggest he wear an Elizabethan collar, a protective collar named for its similarity to the fashion of Elizabeth I's reign. This large, cone-shaped collar will prevent your Pug from licking off the medication and bothering the affected area. He will probably hate this clumsy device and seem very miserable, but try to get him to keep it on. Otherwise,

Squeeze eye ointment into the lower lid.

the wound will take much longer to heal and he will
risk serious infection.

Common Problems

ALLERGIES

Like people, dogs have allergic reactions of varying
degrees of seriousness. Again, because of the nature
of their air passages, flat-faced dogs tend to be more
affected than those with longer muzzles. Allergies can
manifest themselves as multiple lumps appearing
under the skin, or by swelling of the areas around the
eyes and the muzzle. The latter in particular requires
fast action, for the exterior swelling is matched by
internal swelling, which can close off the air passages.

Allergies can be caused by an almost endless number
of allergens (agents): bee stings, airborne pollen, fleas,
dust, woolens. An allergic reaction is essentially caused
by an overreaction of the immune system. The first
time your dog is exposed to an allergen to which he is
susceptible, there will probably be no observable reaction. The second exposure will result in mild reaction.
With subsequent exposures, the reactions will become
increasingly severe until a danger point is reached.
What can be done about it?

Chances are that your veterinarian, being familiar with
a broad range of local patients, will be able to guess at
what allergen is affecting your dog. Then an appropriate antigen can be administered in the form of pills or
injections.

Allergic reactions to immunizations are not unusual in
Pugs. Owners should stay in the veterinary clinic for at
least fifteen minutes after the shots are administered,
just in case such a reaction does occur.

DIARRHEA

Diarrhea occurs most commonly after your Pug has
eaten something he shouldn't. The best treatment is to
feed your Pug a bland diet for the next twenty-four
hours, perhaps mixing rice with his regular food. If the

diarrhea persists, call your veterinarian. Though diarrhea is usually just an upset tummy, it can be a symptom of a more serious problem.

You must also make sure your Pug isn't getting dehydrated, a condition to which puppies are especially prone. Pull up the skin to check for dehydration—if it feels elastic and bounces back, your Pug is okay. If, on the other hand, the skin feels dry and stiff, call your veterinarian at once. Dehydration is a dangerous condition that needs immediate treatment in the form of nutrients administered intravenously.

VOMITING

Like diarrhea, vomiting usually signals an upset stomach and should be treated with a mild diet. Monitor your Pug and call your veterinarian immediately if it happens frequently and your Pug displays other symptoms such as fever or lethargy. Likewise, if the vomitus is bloody, contact your vet as soon as possible.

Emergencies and First Aid

BLEEDING

Apply pressure on the wound with your hand, or with a clean towel if available. When the bleeding has stopped, clean the area with a damp clean towel. If the wound is large, get the dog to a veterinarian, who can suture it if necessary.

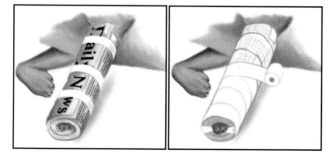

Make a temporary splint by wrapping the leg in firm casing, then bandaging it.

BROKEN BONES

Immobilize a broken bone with a makeshift splint on your way to an emergency care facility. A rolled-up

83

newspaper works well for this purpose. Roll sections of newspaper around the injured limb, and secure with tape or bandage.

CHOKING

Most dogs, and especially short-faced dogs, will at some time get something stuck in their throats—a

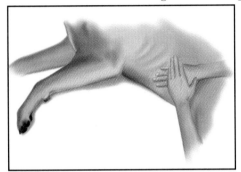

chunk of food, a chewed-off piece of a toy, a piece of rawhide. The symptoms will be apparent: extreme discomfort, gasping for breath, choking sounds, coughing and usually a glazed or frantic look.

If these symptoms are observed, open your Pug's

Applying abdominal thrusts can save a choking dog.

mouth wide, reach a finger down into his throat as far as possible, and try to remove the blockage. If you cannot reach it, or if no such blockage is apparent, rush the dog to the vet as quickly as possible. In most cases, you will be able to remove the obstruction yourself.

Care should also be taken to try to prevent Pugsy from chewing on or swallowing any object that might get stuck in his throat. This includes large chunks of food, especially meat, pieces of a chewing toy (many are made from compressed particles, and these should not be offered), or any object small enough to swallow but large enough to get jammed in the throat and block the windpipe. For chewing toys, which are good for your Pug's teeth and satisfying to his instincts, choose properly treated rawhide, nylon "bones," or anything unlikely to break apart. When a toy begins to get ragged from chewing, replace it with a new toy and throw the old one away.

HEAT STROKE

Heat stroke occurs when a dog has overheated. Symptoms include rapid panting, vomiting, and collapse. You need to cool the affected dog down immediately, but not drastically. Wrap him in cold towels or soak him with cool, not cold, water.

Never leave your Pug in a car on a warm sunny day, even with the windows open. Even a short errand could be unexpectedly prolonged, and you risk putting your Pug's life in danger.

Pugs have a natural inclination to taste just about everything they come in contact with, so it's up to you to make sure dangerous substances are out of their reach.

Poisons

As we've mentioned before, the Pug has a voracious appetite, which can get him into trouble in more ways than one. His initial reaction to just about anything is to taste it, (and keep tasting it!) so not only must we watch his diet, but we must also be careful to keep any and all dangerous substances out of his reach.

Some of the many household substances harmful to your dog.

The most likely poison to cause harm is antifreeze, which seems to taste delicious to dogs who will drink it if they can. Another danger, surprisingly, is chocolate. Dogs, like people, love chocolate (cats do not), but a dog's digestive system works differently and cannot digest chocolate properly. Keep chocolate away from your

Pug, as even a small amount of chocolate can be dangerous for a small dog.

In addition, be sure to keep all household cleaners, medicines, gardening products and automotive supplies well out of reach of your Pug. Make sure your house and garden are free of poisonous plants, including hydrangea, daffodil, oleander and marigold.

Symptoms of poisoning include, vomiting, salivation and convulsions. If you suspect your Pug has been poisoned, call your veterinarian immediately. If you cannot reach your vet, call the National Animal Poison Control Center at (900) 680-0000.

WILD ANIMALS

If you live in a warm climate or close to water, your Pug will eventually encounter some local wildlife. As Pugs are noted for their endless curiosity and fulsome appetite, they will investigate anything in their territory that moves and will probably try to eat it.

TOADS

Toads are poisonous and can cause heart failure in a dog. Their poison is ejected from large salivary glands behind their eyes; a dog who has ingested one will produce frothy white saliva, urinate and defecate and have watery eyes. As soon as such symptoms are noticed, get a hose and direct a flow of water into the dog's mouth for a full five minutes. After the water treatment, Pugsy should be fed a cup of milk, preferably whole milk, using a roasting baster to get it down if necessary. And, of course, call your vet as soon as possible.

BEE STINGS

Bee stings have been found to cause a reaction characterized by swelling of the face and air passages. These should be handled immediately by an injection or an antihistamine. If you expect to encounter bees, it is wise to carry an antihistamine with you for emergency use. Your vet can either furnish this medication with dosage information, or advise you what to buy over the counter.

Snakes are the most dangerous of all. The bites of cottonmouths, water moccasins, rattlers and coral snakes are often fatal. A dog suspected of receiving a snakebite should be rushed to the vet and, if at all possible, the snake should be identified so that the correct antidote can be given. A snakebite will normally leave two puncture wounds on the skin, and will cause swelling around the eyes and muzzle similar to an allergic reaction. Also, if a snakebite is suspected, one should immediately turn up the dog's upper lip and examine its color. A poisonous bite will almost immediately turn the lip color to black or dark purple. Be familiar with the appearance of snakes in your area. Nonpoisonous snakes are generally harmless, and will, as a rule, stay well away from domestic pets.

Problems Particular to Pugs

Although Pugs are subject to all the ailments of the canine species, there are a few common ailments that every Pug owner should be on the lookout for. These are: (1) mange, (2) entropion, and (3) knee problems (luxated patella). Chances are fairly good that your Pug will have or acquire one or more of these.

MANGE

Mange comes in two forms. In Pugs, the most common form and the easiest to deal with is demodectic mange (also known as red or puppy mange). It usually occurs between the ages of four and ten months but can occur as late as eighteen months. Mange is a mite. It is normally present on

An Elizabethan collar keeps your dog from licking a fresh wound.

most dogs but is kept in check by the dog's immune system. Any traumatic event, such as cutting teeth, an airplane trip, the first season or "heat" (in the female), or even a loud noise, can lower the natural immunity and cause the mites to multiply and become virulent. Spots of hair loss will occur which, if unattended, will be followed by skin eruptions and secondary bacterial infections.

At its onset, your Pug may look a bit "moth-eaten," with small spots of thin hair or no hair at all. It is important to catch this condition early and get your puppy to the veterinary clinic at once for a confirming diagnosis and treatment. Although some cases will clear up by themselves, most vets recommend "dipping" weekly over a period of three to six weeks.

If caught early, the effects of the mite infestation is minimal, often almost undetectable, but if noticed late, it can be a serious danger to your Pug. The good news is that, once it has occurred, it seldom returns.

Sarcoptic mange, which is transmittable to humans, is a much more serious problem but happily is quite unusual in Pugs. Demodectic mange is not transmittable to humans.

ENTROPION

The second common problem to which Pugs are heir is entropion, a condition in which eyelashes rub against the surface of the eye, causing irritation which, if left untreated, can lead to blindness. This problem is shared by just about all flat-nosed breeds and is one result of the short muzzle.

A FIRST-AID KIT

Keep a canine first-aid kit on hand for general care and emergencies. Check it periodically to make sure liquids haven't spilled or dried up, and replace medications and materials after they're used. Your kit should include:

Activated charcoal tablets

Adhesive tape
(1 and 2 inches wide)

Antibacterial ointment
(for skin and eyes)

Aspirin (buffered or enteric coated, not Ibuprofen)

Bandages: Gauze rolls (1 and 2 inches wide) and dressing pads

Cotton balls

Diarrhea medicine

Dosing syringe

Hydrogen peroxide (3%)

Petroleum jelly

Rectal thermometer

Rubber gloves

Rubbing alcohol

Scissors

Tourniquet

Towel

Tweezers

Symptoms of entropion are squinting, excessive tear production and staining of the hair below the eyes. If left untreated, the formation of spots of pigment on the eye's surface (pigmentosis) will impair vision. As with other health problems, early detection is important. The condition can be corrected by a minor surgical procedure or can be alleviated or retarded by treating the eyes with a solution of olive oil and cyclosporin (which your veterinarian must prescribe).

As entropion is a genetic defect, dogs who are affected should not be bred. Also, corrective surgery automatically disqualifies a dog from dog shows.

PATELLA LUXATION

The third problem, luxation of the patella (kneecap), has been turning up with some frequency in Pugs, although not nearly as frequently as in larger, heavier breeds. The dog's stifle (knee) is protected by a small bone called a patella, similar to the human kneecap. If, at the point where the upper leg bone (femur) joins the lower leg bone, the femur slips out of place and does not make normal contact at the stifle, then the dog has a luxated patella (trick knee).

Run your hands regularly over your dog to feel for any injuries.

This can be a "sometime" situation, which corrects itself, or a permanent condition. As time goes by, the "sometime" slippage will become permanent unless corrected. This condition can be painful and a nuisance. Corrective surgery is a fairly simple procedure.

PUG DOG ENCEPHALITIS

This is a "breed-specific" disease found only in Pugs. As far as we are aware, this is the *only* disease found exclusively in Pugs. Other breeds may have encephalitis, but the nature of this disease is unique to Pugs.

Encephalitis is basically an inflammation of the brain; meningitis is an inflammation of the brain's coverings (meninges). Pug encephalitis usually involves both the brain and its outer membranes. The causes of this inflammation are numerous and some are unknown. Bacteria, viruses, fungi and other organisms have been identified. It can be caused by the immune system making a "mistake," by either failing to react to the infecting agent or by mistaking the brain for a foreign agent.

Pug Encephalitis is a new disease or, perhaps more accurately, a newly discovered one. It was first identified in California in the 1960s, and has since spread to all parts of the United States as well as to other countries. Because it is difficult to diagnose, it is probably more widespread than realized because it is frequently misdiagnosed. In fact, a firm diagnosis can be made only by autopsy—too late to take remedial action.

There is reason to believe that a predisposition to this disease is inherited, as data so far assembled indicates the likelihood that littermates or close relatives of an affected Pug are also prone to it. Because this is a new and not fully analyzed disease, breeders are just beginning to have a full realization of its effect on Pugs, and are withdrawing any of their "at risk" Pugs from their breeding program.

Symptoms include seizures, circling, pressing the head against a firm object (probably indicating headache), weakness on one side of the body, faulty eyesight and sometimes neck pain. Ordinary tests usually come back normal, although there is sometimes a rise in the white blood cells of the spinal fluid. These symptoms become progressively worse; however, a temporary improvement may occur spontaneously or as a result of medicating with prednisone.

There are no known cases in which a Pug has survived this disease. As with any new disease, it will take years for veterinary researchers to gather enough data to understand PDE, and much depends on the cooperation of Pug owners everywhere. If this happens to your Pug, it is very important that you ask your vet to contact his or her veterinary college and request guidance on what should be done. You must also notify your Pug's breeder.

HEMIVERTIBRAE

That's a big word which simply means "half of a vertebrae." This appears to be an inherited defect. It has generally escaped serious attention until a few years ago. It is a disease Pugs share with Bulldogs, French Bulldogs and Boston Terriers.

The least technical definition of HV is "a congenital vertebral malformation produced by a failure of fusion of the left and right ossification centers of the vertebral bodies." In plain English it boils down to this: As a dog's skeleton matures, one or more of the vertebra does not form correctly, which may result in curvature of the spine and compression of the spinal cord. This in turn causes loss of feeling and/or control of the rear limbs. The unfortunate thing about HV is that it is undetectable until a puppy is six to eight months old and has gone to its new home. While any vertebrae in the spinal column can be affected by HV, it affects the dog only if it occurs in those vertebrae at the base of the neck.

Check your dog's teeth frequently and brush them regularly.

One lady who had experience with HV has written,

> Bijou was a beautiful puppy, the child of two champions and I had high hopes for her. (Shortly after) six months, it became apparent that something was wrong. She had a tendency to pace, which soon became an inability to trot properly at all. By the time she was eight months old, she had lost most feeling in her hindquarters and was unable to take even a few steps without

falling over. Her hind feet would bleed after any exercise because she would drag them while bringing them forward. There did not seem to be any pain involved, but she was distressed at not being able to run with the others or to jump, and she was not clean.

HV was diagnosed by X ray. Surgery was apparently out of the question as few vets would be willing to invade the spine of a still growing puppy. With little guidance, the owner of Bijou tried many cures, including acupuncture and homeopathy. After about a month, Bijou showed signs of improvement and today, at age five, she can lead a fairly normal life, though her movement is restricted.

An older Pug deserves special care and attention, though she may not be as bouncy or energetic as she was in her younger years.

Since Bijou's illness, several more such cases have come to light, all with the same symptoms. Not all recovered, and a few had to be put down because the disease had progressed beyond a tolerable point.

As there is no known way to predict whether a puppy will develop HV, and there is no generally accepted method of treatment, the only preventive measures that can be taken are to provide the Pug's breeder with the dog's medical history, and to rely on his/her integrity in not repeating a breeding that produced the affected Pug. This, of course, offers the owner little consolation.

As noted above, Pugs are subject to most diseases and conditions found in other canines, but those noted above seem to be the most prevalent in the breed today. As we give our Pugs their daily brushing, nose fold and ears check, we should also be alert to any symptoms of the problems noted above, as well as any other abnormalities. And when in doubt, see your vet without delay.

Old Age and Euthanasia

We like to think of a Pug as a fun-loving, bouncy, vigorous, bright-eyed little personality bounding through the house with all the exuberance of youth. In his youth, he will be just that. But when you acquire a Pug, you are making a long-term commitment that will take you through his puppyhood, his prime, his advancing years and possibly his senility. Throughout, he will remain your adoring friend who places complete trust in you to take care of his needs. He will not expect to be neglected when he no longer wants, or is able, to romp.

A well-cared-for Pug will live on the average from twelve to fifteen years. From eight or nine years on, you will see a gradual decline in his faculties. Some suffering from arthritis, some deterioration in the liver function, failing eyesight, and some loss of bladder control are all possibilities. The quality of his life will come into question, and you will have to decide if taking major or even heroic measures to prolong his life is for his benefit or for yours. The decision must favor his benefit, for you will lose him sooner or later. When the time comes—when your vet tells you that he is suffering and will not recover—the humane thing to turn to is euthanasia. It will be a very difficult decision for you to make but one you cannot avoid, and you must expect to have some feelings of guilt even though you are doing the best thing for your dog.

When that time comes, try to persuade your veterinarian to come to your home to administer the dose. If that's not an option, make sure you accompany your Pug to the vet. Stay with him while the veterinarian administers an overdose of anesthetic. Talk to him comfortingly and gently, and make his last moments as pleasant and full of love as possible.

Your Happy, Healthy Pet

Your Dog's Name _____

Name on Your Dog's Pedigree (if your dog has one) _____
_____

Where Your Dog Came From _____
_____

Your Dog's Birthday _____

Your Dog's Veterinarian

    Name _____

    Address _____

    Phone Number_____

    Emergency Number_____

Your Dog's Health

    Vaccines

    type _____ date given _____

    type _____ date given _____

    type _____ date given _____

    type _____ date given _____

    Heartworm

    date tested _____ type used_____ start date _____

Your Dog's License Number_____

Groomer's Name and Number _____

Dogsitter/Walker's Name and Number_____

Awards Your Dog Has Won

    Award _____ date earned _____

    Award _____ date earned _____

part three

Enjoying
your
Dog

chapter 8

Basic
Training

by Ian Dunbar, Ph.D., MRCVS

Training is the jewel in the crown—the most important aspect of doggy husbandry. There is no more important variable influencing dog behavior and temperament than the dog's education: A well-trained, well-behaved and good-natured puppydog is always a joy to live with, but an untrained and un-civilized dog can be a perpetual nightmare. Moreover, deny the dog an education and she will not have the opportunity to fulfill her own canine potential; neither will she have the ability to communicate effectively with her human companions.

Luckily, modern psychological training methods are easy, efficient, effective and, above all, considerably dog-friendly and user-friendly.

Doggy education is as simple as it is enjoyable. But before you can have a good time play-training with your new dog, you have to learn what to do and how to do it. There is no bigger variable influencing the success of dog training than the *owner's* experience and expertise. *Before you embark on the dog's education, you must first educate yourself.*

Basic Training for Owners

Ideally, basic owner training should begin well *before* you select your dog. Find out all you can about your chosen breed first, then master rudimentary training and handling skills. If you already have your puppy-dog, owner training is a dire emergency—the clock is ticking! Especially for puppies, the first few weeks at home are the most important and influential days in the dog's life. Indeed, the cause of most adolescent and adult problems may be traced back to the initial days the pup explores her new home. This is the time to establish the *status quo*—to teach the puppydog how you would like her to behave and so prevent otherwise quite predictable problems.

In addition to consulting breeders and breed books such as this one (which understandably have a positive breed bias), seek out as many pet owners with your breed as you can find. Good points are obvious. What you want to find out are the breed-specific *problems,* so you can nip them in the bud. In particular, you should talk to owners with *adolescent* dogs and make a list of all anticipated problems. Most important, *test drive* at least half a dozen adolescent and adult dogs of your breed yourself. An 8-week-old puppy is deceptively easy to handle, but she will acquire adult size, speed and strength in just four months, so you should learn now what to prepare for.

Puppy and pet dog training classes offer a convenient venue to locate pet owners and observe dogs in action. For a list of suitable trainers in your area, contact the Association of Pet Dog Trainers (see chapter 13). You may also begin your basic owner training by observing other owners in class. Watch as many classes and test drive as many dogs as possible. Select an upbeat, dog-friendly, people-friendly, fun-and-games, puppydog pet training class to learn the ropes. Also, watch training videos and read training books. You must find out what to do and how to do it *before* you have to do it.

Principles of Training

Most people think training comprises teaching the dog to do things such as sit, speak and roll over, but even a 4-week-old pup knows how to do these things already. Instead, the first step in training involves teaching the dog human words for each dog behavior and activity and for each aspect of the dog's environment. That way you, the owner, can more easily participate in the dog's domestic education by directing her to perform specific actions appropriately, that is, at the right time, in the right place and so on. Training opens communication channels, enabling an educated dog to at least understand her owner's requests.

In addition to teaching a dog *what* we want her to do, it is also necessary to teach her *why* she should do what we ask. Indeed, 95 percent of training revolves around motivating the dog *to want to do* what we want. Dogs often understand what their owners want; they just don't see the point of doing it—especially when the owner's repetitively boring and seemingly senseless instructions are totally at odds with much more pressing and exciting doggy distractions. It is not so much the dog that is being stubborn or dominant; rather, it is the owner who has failed to acknowledge the dog's needs and feelings and to approach training from the dog's point of view.

The Meaning of Instructions

The secret to successful training is learning how to use training lures to predict or prompt specific behaviors—to coax the dog to do what you want *when* you want. Any highly valued object (such as a treat or toy) may be used as a lure, which the dog will follow with her eyes and nose. Moving the lure in specific ways entices the dog to move her nose, head and entire body in specific ways. In fact, by learning the art of manipulating various lures, it is possible to teach the dog to assume virtually any body position and perform any action. Once you have control over the expression of the dog's behaviors and can elicit any body position or behavior at will, you can easily teach the dog to perform on request.

Teach your dog words for each activity she needs to know, like down.

Tell your dog what you want her to do, use a lure to entice her to respond correctly, then profusely praise and maybe reward her once she performs the desired action. For example, verbally request "Tina, sit!" while you move a squeaky toy upwards and backwards over the dog's muzzle (lure-movement and hand signal), smile knowingly as she looks up (to follow the lure) and sits down (as a result of canine anatomical engineering), then praise her to distraction ("Gooood Tina!"). Squeak the toy, offer a training treat and give your dog and yourself a pat on the back.

Being able to elicit desired responses over and over enables the owner to reward the dog over and over. Consequently, the dog begins to think training is fun. For example, the more the dog is rewarded for sitting, the more she enjoys sitting. Eventually the dog comes to realize that, whereas most sitting is appreciated, sitting immediately upon request usually prompts especially enthusiastic praise and a slew of high-level rewards. The dog begins to sit on cue much of the time, showing that she is starting to grasp the meaning of the owner's verbal request and hand signal.

Why Comply?

Most dogs enjoy initial lure-reward training and are only too happy to comply with their owners' wishes. Unfortunately, repetitive drilling without appreciative feedback tends to diminish the dog's enthusiasm until she eventually fails to see the point of complying anymore. Moreover, as the dog approaches adolescence she becomes more easily distracted as she develops other interests. Lengthy sessions with repetitive exercises tend to bore and demotivate both parties. If it's not fun, the owner doesn't do it and neither does the dog.

Integrate training into your dog's life: The greater number of training sessions each day and the *shorter* they are, the more willingly compliant your dog will

become. Make sure to have a short (just a few seconds) training interlude before every enjoyable canine activity. For example, ask your dog to sit to greet people, to sit before you throw her Frisbee and to sit for her supper. Really, sitting is no different from a canine "Please."

To train your dog, you need gentle hands, a loving heart and a good attitude.

Also, include numerous short training interludes during every enjoyable canine pastime, for example, when playing with the dog or when she is running in the park. In this fashion, doggy distractions may be effectively converted into rewards for training. Just as all games have rules, fun becomes training . . . and training becomes fun.

Eventually, rewards actually become unnecessary to continue motivating your dog. If trained with consideration and kindness, performing the desired behaviors will become self-rewarding and, in a sense, your dog will motivate herself. Just as it is not necessary to reward a human companion during an enjoyable walk in the park, or following a game of tennis, it is hardly necessary to reward our best friend—the dog—for walking by our side or while playing fetch. Human company during enjoyable activities is reward enough for most dogs.

Even though your dog has become self-motivating, it's still good to praise and pet her a lot and offer rewards once in a while, especially for a good job well done. And if for no other reason, praising and rewarding others is good for the human heart.

PUNISHMENT

Without a doubt, lure-reward training is by far the best way to teach: Entice your dog to do what you want and then reward her for doing so. Unfortunately, a human shortcoming is to take the good for granted and to moan and groan at the bad. Specifically, the dog's many good behaviors are ignored while the owner focuses on punishing the dog for making mistakes. In extreme cases, instruction is *limited* to punishing mistakes made by a trainee dog, child, employee or husband, even though it has been proven punishment training is notoriously inefficient and ineffective and is decidedly unfriendly and combative. It teaches the dog that training is a drag, almost as quickly as it teaches the dog to dislike her trainer. Why treat our best friends like our worst enemies?

Punishment training is also much more laborious and time consuming. Whereas it takes only a finite amount of time to teach a dog what to chew, for example, it takes much, much longer to punish the dog for each and every mistake. Remember, *there is only one right way!* So why not teach that right way from the outset?!

To make matters worse, punishment training causes severe lapses in the dog's reliability. Since it is obviously impossible to punish the dog each and every time she misbehaves, the dog quickly learns to distinguish between those times when she must comply (so as to avoid impending punishment) and those times when she need not comply, because punishment is impossible. Such times include when the dog is off leash and 6 feet away, when the owner is otherwise engaged (talking to a friend, watching television, taking a shower, tending to the baby or chatting on the telephone) or when the dog is left at home alone.

Instances of misbehavior will be numerous when the owner is away, because even when the dog complied in the owner's looming presence, she did so unwillingly. The dog was forced to act against her will, rather than molding her will to want to please. Hence, when the owner is absent, not only does the dog know she need not comply, she simply does not want to. Again, the trainee is not a stubborn vindictive beast, but rather the trainer has failed to teach. Punishment training invariably creates unpredictable Jekyll and Hyde behavior.

Trainer's Tools

Many training books extol the virtues of a vast array of training paraphernalia and electronic and metallic gizmos, most of which are designed for canine restraint, correction and punishment, rather than for actual facilitation of doggy education. In reality, most effective training tools are not found in stores; they come from within ourselves. In addition to a willing dog, all you really need is a functional human brain, gentle hands, a loving heart and a good attitude.

In terms of equipment, all dogs do require a quality buckle collar to sport dog tags and to attach the leash (for safety and to comply with local leash laws). Hollow chew toys (like Kongs or sterilized longbones) and a dog bed or collapsible crate are musts for housetraining. Three additional tools are required:

1. specific lures (training treats and toys) to predict and prompt specific desired behaviors;

2. rewards (praise, affection, training treats and toys) to reinforce for the dog what a lot of fun it all is; and

3. knowledge—how to convert the dog's favorite activities and games (potential distractions to training) into "life-rewards," which may be employed to facilitate training.

The most powerful of these is *knowledge.* Education is the key! Watch training classes, participate in training classes, watch videos, read books, enjoy play-training with your dog and then your dog will say "Please," and your dog will say "Thank you!"

Housetraining

If dogs were left to their own devices, certainly they would chew, dig and bark for entertainment and then no doubt highlight a few areas of their living space with sprinkles of urine, in much the same way we decorate by hanging pictures. Consequently, when we ask a dog to live with us, we must teach her *where* she may dig, *where* she may perform her toilet duties, *what* she may chew and *when* she may bark. After all, when left at home alone for many hours, we cannot expect the dog to amuse herself by completing crosswords or watching the soaps on TV!

Also, it would be decidedly unfair to keep the house rules a secret from the dog, and then get angry and punish the poor critter for inevitably transgressing rules she did not even know existed. Remember: Without adequate education and guidance, the dog will be forced to establish her own rules—doggy rules—and most probably will be at odds with the owner's view of domestic living.

Since most problems develop during the first few days the dog is at home, prospective dog owners must be certain they are quite clear about the principles of housetraining *before* they get a dog. Early misbehaviors quickly become established as the *status quo*—

becoming firmly entrenched as hard-to-break bad habits, which set the precedent for years to come. Make sure to teach your dog good habits right from the start. Good habits are just as hard to break as bad ones!

Ideally, when a new dog comes home, try to arrange for someone to be present as much as possible during the first few days (for adult dogs) or weeks for puppies. With only a little forethought, it is surprisingly easy to find a puppy sitter, such as a retired person, who would be willing to eat from your refrigerator and watch your television while keeping an eye on the newcomer to encourage the dog to play with chew toys and to ensure she goes outside on a regular basis.

POTTY TRAINING

To teach the dog where to relieve herself:

1. never let her make a single mistake;

2. let her know where you want her to go; and

3. handsomely reward her for doing so: "GOOOOOOOD DOG!!!" liver treat, liver treat, liver treat!

Preventing Mistakes

A single mistake is a training disaster, since it heralds many more in future weeks. And each time the dog soils the house, this further reinforces the dog's unfortunate preference for an indoor, carpeted toilet. *Do not let an unhousetrained dog have full run of the house.*

When you are away from home, or cannot pay full attention, confine the dog to an area where elimination is appropriate, such as an outdoor run or, better still, a small, comfortable indoor kennel with access to an outdoor run. When confined in this manner, most dogs will naturally housetrain themselves.

If that's not possible, confine the dog to an area, such as a utility room, kitchen, basement or garage, where elimination may not be desired in the long run but as an interim measure it is certainly preferable to doing it all around the house. Use newspaper to cover the floor of the dog's day room. The newspaper may be used to soak up the urine and to wrap up and dispose of the feces. Once your dog develops a preferred spot for eliminating, it is only necessary to cover that part of the floor with newspaper. The smaller papered area may then be moved (only a little each day) towards the door to the outside. Thus the dog will develop the tendency to go to the door when she needs to relieve herself.

Never confine an unhousetrained dog to a crate for long periods. Doing so would force the dog to soil the crate and ruin its usefulness as an aid for housetraining (see the following discussion).

Teaching Where

In order to teach your dog where you would like her to do her business, you have to be there to direct the proceedings—an obvious, yet often neglected, fact of life. In order to be there

to teach the dog *where* to go, you need to know *when* she needs to go. Indeed, the success of housetraining depends on the owner's ability to predict these times. Certainly, a regular feeding schedule will facilitate prediction somewhat, but there is nothing like "loading the deck" and influencing the timing of the outcome yourself!

Whenever you are at home, make sure the dog is under constant supervision and/or confined to a small

The first few weeks at home are the most important and influential in your dog's life.

area. If already well trained, simply instruct the dog to lie down in her bed or basket. Alternatively, confine the dog to a crate (doggy den) or tie-down (a short, 18-inch lead that can be clipped to an eye hook in the baseboard near her bed). Short-term close confinement strongly inhibits urination and defecation, since the dog does not want to soil her sleeping area. Thus, when you release the puppydog each hour, she will definitely need to urinate immediately and defecate every third or fourth hour. Keep the dog confined to her doggy den and take her to her intended toilet area each hour, every hour and on the hour.

When taking your dog outside, instruct her to sit quietly before opening the door—she will soon learn to sit by the door when she needs to go out!

Teaching Why

Being able to predict when the dog needs to go enables the owner to be on the spot to praise and reward the dog. Each hour, hurry the dog to the intended toilet area in the yard, issue the appropriate instruction ("Go pee!" or "Go poop!"), then give the dog three to four minutes to produce. Praise and offer a couple of training treats when successful. The treats are important because many people fail to praise their dogs with feeling . . . and housetraining is hardly the time for understatement. So either loosen up and enthusiastically praise that dog: "Wuzzzer-wuzzer-wuzzer, hoooser good wuffer den? Hoooo went pee for Daddy?" Or say "Good dog!" as best you can and offer the treats for effect.

Following elimination is an ideal time for a spot of play-training in the yard or house. Also, an empty dog may be allowed greater freedom around the house for the next half hour or so, just as long as you keep an eye out to make sure she does not get into other kinds of mischief. If you are preoccupied and cannot pay full attention, confine the dog to her doggy den once more to enjoy a peaceful snooze or to play with her many chew toys.

If your dog does not eliminate within the allotted time outside—no biggie! Back to her doggy den, and then try again after another hour.

As I own large dogs, I always feel more relaxed walking an empty dog, knowing that I will not need to finish our stroll weighted down with bags of feces!

Beware of falling into the trap of walking the dog to get her to eliminate. The good ol' dog walk is such an enormous highlight in the dog's life that it represents the single biggest potential reward in domestic dogdom. However, when in a hurry, or during inclement weather, many owners abruptly terminate the walk the moment the dog has done her business. This, in effect, severely punishes the dog for doing the right thing, in the right place at the right time. Consequently, many dogs become strongly inhibited from eliminating outdoors because they know it will signal an abrupt end to an otherwise thoroughly enjoyable walk.

Instead, instruct the dog to relieve herself in the yard prior to going for a walk. If you follow the above instructions, most dogs soon learn to eliminate on cue. As soon as the dog eliminates, praise (and offer a treat or two)—"Good dog! Let's go walkies!" Use the walk as a reward for eliminating in the yard. If the dog does not go, put her back in her doggy den and think about a walk later on. You will find with a "No feces—no walk" policy, your dog will become one of the fastest defecators in the business.

If you do not have a backyard, instruct the dog to eliminate right outside your front door prior to the walk. Not only will this facilitate clean up and disposal of the feces in your own trash can but, also, the walk may again be used as a colossal reward.

CHEWING AND BARKING

Short-term close confinement also teaches the dog that occasional quiet moments are a reality of domestic living. Your puppydog is extremely impressionable during her first few weeks at home. Regular confinement at this time soon exerts a calming influence over the dog's personality. Remember, once the dog is housetrained and calmer, there will be a whole lifetime ahead for the dog to enjoy full run of the house and garden. On the other hand, by letting the newcomer have unrestricted access to the entire household and allowing her to run willy-nilly, she will most certainly develop a bunch of behavior problems in short order, no doubt necessitating confinement later in life. It would not be fair to remedially restrain and confine a dog you have trained, through neglect, to run free.

When confining the dog, make sure she always has an impressive array of suitable chew toys. Kongs and sterilized longbones (both readily available from pet stores) make the best chew toys, since they are hollow and may be stuffed with treats to heighten the dog's interest. For example, by stuffing the little hole at the top of a Kong with a small piece of freeze-dried liver, the dog will not want to leave it alone.

Remember, treats do not have to be junk food and they certainly should not represent extra calories. Rather, treats should be part of each dog's regular

daily diet: Some food may be served in the dog's bowl for breakfast and dinner, some food may be used as training treats, and some food may be used for stuffing chew toys. I regularly stuff my dogs' many Kongs with different shaped biscuits and kibble.

Make sure your puppy has suitable chew toys.

The kibble seems to fall out fairly easily, as do the oval-shaped biscuits, thus rewarding the dog instantaneously for checking out the chew toys. The bone-shaped biscuits fall out after a while, rewarding the dog for worrying at the chew toy. But the triangular biscuits never come out. They remain inside the Kong as lures, maintaining the dog's fascination with her chew toy. To further focus the dog's interest, I always make sure to flavor the triangular biscuits by rubbing them with a little cheese or freeze-dried liver.

To teach come, call your dog, open your arms as a welcoming signal, wave a toy or a treat and praise for every step in your direction.

If stuffed chew toys are reserved especially for times the dog is confined, the puppydog will soon learn to enjoy quiet moments in her doggy den and she will quickly develop a chew-toy habit— a good habit! This is a simple *autoshaping* process; all the owner has to do is set up the situation and the dog all but trains herself— easy and effective. Even when the dog is given run of the house, her first inclination will be to indulge her rewarding chew-toy habit rather than destroy less-attractive household articles, such as curtains, car-pets, chairs and compact disks. Similarly, a chew-toy chewer will be less inclined to scratch and chew herself excessively. Also, if the dog busies herself as a recreational chewer, she will be less inclined to develop into a recreational barker or digger when left at home alone.

Stuff a number of chew toys whenever the dog is left confined and remove the extra-special-tasting treats when you return. Your dog will now amuse herself with her chew toys before falling asleep and then resume playing with her chew toys when she expects you to return. Since most owner-absent misbehavior happens right after you leave and right before your expected return, your puppydog will now be conveniently preoccupied with her chew toys at these times.

Come and Sit

Most puppies will happily approach virtual-ly anyone, whether called or not; that is, until they collide with adolescence and develop other more important doggy interests, such as sniffing a multiplicity of exquisite odors on the grass. Your mission, Mr./Ms. Owner, is to teach and reward the pup for coming reliably, willingly and happily when called—and you have just three months to get it done. Unless adequately reinforced, your puppy's tendency to approach people will self-destruct by adolescence.

Call your dog ("Tina, come!"), open your arms (and maybe squat down) as a welcoming signal, waggle a treat or toy as a lure and reward the puppydog when she comes running. Do not wait to praise the dog until she reaches you—she may come 95 percent of the way and then run off after some distraction. Instead, praise the dog's *first* step towards you and continue praising enthusiastically for *every* step she takes in your direction.

When the rapidly approaching puppy dog is three lengths away from impact, instruct her to sit ("Tina, sit!") and hold the lure in front of you in an outstretched hand to prevent her from hitting you midchest and knocking you flat on your back! As Tina decelerates to nose the lure, move the treat upwards and backwards just over her muzzle with an upwards motion of your extended arm (palm-upwards). As the dog looks up to follow the lure, she will sit down (if she jumps up, you are holding the lure too high). Praise the dog for sitting. Move backwards and call her again. Repeat this many times over, always praising when Tina comes and sits; on occasion, reward her.

For the first couple of trials, use a training treat both as a lure to entice the dog to come and sit and as a reward for doing so. Thereafter, try to use different items as lures and rewards. For example, lure the dog with a Kong or Frisbee but reward her with a food treat. Or lure the dog with a food treat but pat her and throw a tennis ball as a reward. After just a few repetitions, dispense with the lures and rewards; the dog will begin to respond willingly to your verbal requests and hand signals just for the prospect of praise from your heart and affection from your hands.

Instruct every family member, friend and visitor how to get the dog to come and sit. Invite people over for a series of pooch parties; do not keep the pup a secret—let other people enjoy this puppy, and let the pup enjoy other people. Puppydog parties are not only fun, they easily attract a lot of people to help *you* train *your* dog. Unless you teach your dog how to meet people, that is, to sit for greetings, no doubt the dog will resort to jumping up. Then you and the visitors will get annoyed, and the dog will be punished. This is not fair. *Send out those invitations for puppy parties and teach your dog to be mannerly and socially acceptable.*

Even though your dog quickly masters obedient recalls in the house, her reliability may falter when playing in the backyard or local park. Ironically, it is *the owner* who has unintentionally trained the dog *not* to respond in these instances. By allowing the dog to play and run around and otherwise have a good time, but then to call the dog to put her on leash to take her home, the dog quickly learns playing is fun but training is a drag. Thus, playing in the park becomes a severe distraction, which works against training. Bad news!

Instead, whether playing with the dog off leash or on leash, request her to come at frequent intervals—say, every minute or so. On most occasions, praise and pet the dog for a few seconds while she is sitting, then tell her to go play again. For especially fast recalls, offer a couple of training treats and take the time to praise and pet the dog enthusiastically before releasing her. The dog will learn that coming when called is not necessarily the end of the play session, and neither is it the end of the world; rather, it signals an enjoyable, quality time-out with the owner before resuming play once more. In fact, playing in the park now becomes a very effective life-reward, which works to facilitate training by reinforcing each obedient and timely recall. Good news!

Sit, Down, Stand and Rollover

Teaching the dog a variety of body positions is easy for owner and dog, impressive for spectators and extremely useful for all. Using lure-reward techniques, it is possible to train several positions at once to verbal commands or hand signals (which impress the socks off onlookers).

Sit and *down*—the two control commands—prevent or resolve nearly a hundred behavior problems. For example, if the dog happily and obediently sits or lies down when requested, she cannot jump on visitors, dash out the front door, run around and chase her tail, pester other dogs, harass cats or annoy family, friends or strangers. Additionally, "Sit" or "Down" are the best emergency commands for off-leash control.

It is easier to teach and maintain a reliable sit than maintain a reliable recall. *Sit* is the purest and simplest of commands—either the dog is sitting or she is not. If there is any change of circumstances or potential danger in the park, for example, simply instruct the dog to sit. If she sits, you have a number of options: Allow the dog to resume playing when she is safe, walk up and put the dog on leash or call the dog. The dog will be much more likely to come when called if she has already acknowledged her compliance by sitting. If the dog does not sit in the park—train her to!

Stand and *rollover-stay* are the two positions for examining the dog. Your veterinarian will love you to distraction if you take a little time to teach the dog to stand still and roll over and play possum. Also, your vet bills will be smaller because it will take the veterinarian less time to examine your dog. The rollover-stay is an especially useful command and is really just a variation of the down-stay: Whereas the dog lies prone in the traditional down, she lies supine in the rollover-stay.

As with teaching come and sit, the training techniques to teach the dog to assume all other body positions on cue are user-friendly and dog-friendly. Simply give the appropriate request, lure the dog into the desired body position using a training treat or toy and then *praise* (and maybe reward) the dog as soon as she complies. Try not to touch the dog to get her to respond. If you teach the dog by guiding her into position, the dog will quickly learn that rump-pressure means sit, for example, but as yet you still have no control over your dog if she is just 6 feet away. It will still be necessary to teach the dog to sit on request. So do not make training a time-consuming two-step process; instead, teach the dog to sit to a verbal request or hand signal from the outset. Once the dog sits willingly when requested, by all means use your hands to pet the dog when she does so.

To teach **down** when the dog is already sitting, say "Tina, down!," hold the lure in one hand (palm down) and lower that hand to the floor between the dog's forepaws. As the dog lowers her head to follow the lure, slowly move the lure away from the dog just a fraction (in front of her paws). The dog will lie down as she stretches her nose forward to follow the lure. Praise the dog when she does so. If the dog stands up, you pulled the lure away too far and too quickly.

When teaching the dog to lie down from the standing position, say "Down" and lower the lure to the floor as before. Once the dog has lowered her forequarters and assumed a play bow, gently and slowly move the lure *towards* the dog between her forelegs. Praise the dog as soon as her rear end plops down.

After just a couple of trials it will be possible to alternate sits and downs and have the dog energetically perform doggy push-ups. Praise the dog a lot, and after half a dozen or so push-ups reward the dog with a training treat or toy. You will notice the more energetically you move your arm—upwards (palm up) to get the dog to sit, and downwards (palm down) to get the dog to lie down—the more energetically the dog responds to your requests. Now try training the dog in silence and you will notice she has also learned to respond to hand signals. Yeah! Not too shabby for the first session.

To teach **stand** from the sitting position, say "Tina, stand," slowly move the lure half a dog-length away from the dog's nose, keeping it at nose level, and praise the dog as she stands to follow the lure. As soon

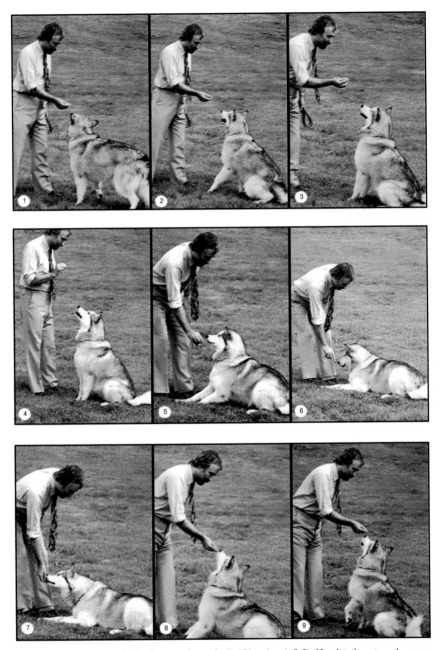

Using a food lure to teach sit, down and stand. 1) "Phoenix, sit." 2) Hand palm upwards, move lure up and back over dog's muzzle. 3) "Good sit, Phoenix!" 4) "Phoenix, down." 5) Hand palm downwards, move lure down to lie between dog's forepaws. 6) "Phoenix, off. Good down, Phoenix!" 7) "Phoenix, sit!" 8) Palm upwards, move lure up and back, keeping it close to dog's muzzle. 9) "Good sit, Phoenix!"

10) *"Phoenix, stand!" 11) Move lure away from dog at nose height, then lower it a tad. 12) "Phoenix, off! Good stand, Phoenix!" 13) "Phoenix, down!" 14) Hand palm downwards, move lure down to lie between dog's forepaws. 15) "Phoenix, off! Good down-stay, Phoenix!" 16) "Phoenix, stand!" 17) Move lure away from dog's muzzle up to nose height. 18) "Phoenix, off! Good stand-stay, Phoenix. Now we'll make the vet and groomer happy!"*

as the dog stands, lower the lure to just beneath the dog's chin to entice her to look down; otherwise she will stand and then sit immediately. To prompt the dog to stand from the down position, move the lure half a dog-length upwards and away from the dog, holding the lure at standing nose height from the floor.

Teaching *rollover* is best started from the down position, with the dog lying on one side, or at least with both hind legs stretched out on the same side. Say "Tina, bang!" and move the lure backwards and alongside the dog's muzzle to her elbow (on the side of her outstretched hind legs). Once the dog looks to the side and backwards, very slowly move the lure upwards to the dog's shoulder and backbone. Tickling the dog in the goolies (groin area) often invokes a reflex-raising of the hind leg as an appeasement gesture, which facilitates the tendency to roll over. If you move the lure too quickly and the dog jumps into the standing position, have patience and start again. As soon as the dog rolls onto her back, keep the lure stationary and mesmerize the dog with a relaxing tummy rub.

To teach *rollover-stay* when the dog is standing or moving, say "Tina, bang!" and give the appropriate hand signal (with index finger pointed and thumb cocked in true Sam Spade fashion), then in one fluid movement lure her to first lie down and then rollover-stay as above.

Teaching the dog to *stay* in each of the above four positions becomes a piece of cake after first teaching the dog not to worry at the toy or treat training lure. This is best accomplished by hand feeding dinner kibble. Hold a piece of kibble firmly in your hand and softly instruct "Off!" Ignore any licking and slobbering *for however long the dog worries at the treat*, but say "Take it!" and offer the kibble *the instant* the dog breaks contact with her muzzle. Repeat this a few times, and then up the ante and insist the dog remove her muzzle for one whole second before offering the kibble. Then progressively refine your criteria and have the dog not touch your hand (or treat) for longer and longer periods on each trial, such as for two seconds, four seconds, then six, ten, fifteen, twenty, thirty seconds and so on.

The dog soon learns: (1) worrying at the treat never gets results, whereas (2) noncontact is often rewarded after a variable time lapse.

Teaching *"Off!"* has many useful applications in its own right. Additionally, instructing the dog not to touch a training lure often produces spontaneous and magical stays. Request the dog to stand-stay, for example, and not to touch the lure. At first set your sights on a short two-second stay before rewarding the dog. (Remember, every long journey begins with a single step.) However, on subsequent trials, gradually and progressively increase the length of stay required to receive a reward. In no time at all your dog will stand calmly for a minute or so.

Relevancy Training

Once you have taught the dog what you expect her to do when requested to come, sit, lie down, stand, rollover and stay, the time is right to teach the dog *why* she should comply with your wishes. The secret is to have many (*many*) extremely short training interludes (two to five seconds each) at numerous (*numerous*) times during the course of the dog's day. Especially work with the dog immediately *before* the dog's good times and *during* the dog's good times. For example, ask your dog to sit and/or lie down each time before opening doors, serving meals, offering treats and tummy rubs; ask the dog to perform a few controlled doggy push-ups before letting her off leash or throwing a tennis ball; and perhaps request the dog to sit-down-sit-stand-down-stand-rollover before inviting her to cuddle on the couch.

Similarly, request the dog to sit many times during play or on walks, and in no time at all the dog will be only too pleased to follow your instructions because she has learned that a compliant response heralds all sorts of goodies. Basically all you are trying to teach the dog is how to say please: "Please throw the tennis ball. Please may I snuggle on the couch."

Remember, it is important to keep training interludes short and to have many short sessions each and every day. The shortest (and most useful) session comprises asking the dog to sit and then go play during a play session. When trained this way, your dog will soon associate training with good times. In fact, the dog may be unable to distinguish between training and good times and, indeed, there should be no distinction. The warped concept that training involves forcing the dog to comply and/or dominating her will is totally at odds with the picture of a truly well-trained dog. In reality, enjoying a game of training with a dog is no different from enjoying a game of backgammon or tennis with a friend; and walking with a dog should be no different from strolling with a spouse, or with buddies on the golf course.

Walk by Your Side

Many people attempt to teach a dog to heel by putting her on a leash and physically correcting the dog when she makes mistakes. There are a number of things seriously wrong with this approach, the first being that most people do not want precision heeling; rather, they simply want the dog to follow or walk by their side. Second, when physically restrained during "training," even though the dog may grudgingly mope by your side when "handcuffed" on leash, let's see what happens when she is off leash. History! The dog is in the next county because she never enjoyed walking with you on leash and you have no control over her off leash. So let's just teach the dog off leash from the outset to *want* to walk with us. Third, if the dog has not been trained to heel, it is a trifle hasty to think about punishing the poor dog for making mistakes and breaking heeling rules she didn't even know existed. This is simply not fair! Surely, if the dog had been adequately taught how to heel, she would seldom make mistakes and hence there would be no need to correct the dog. Remember, each mistake and each correction (punishment) advertise the trainer's inadequacy, not the dog's. The dog is not stubborn, she is not stupid and she is not bad. Even if she were, she would still require training, so let's train her properly.

Let's teach the dog to *enjoy* following us and to *want* to walk by our side off leash. Then it will be easier to teach high-precision off-leash heeling patterns if desired. Before going on outdoor walks, it is necessary to teach the dog not to pull. Then it becomes easy to teach on-leash walking and heeling because the dog already wants to walk with you, she is familiar with the desired walking and heeling positions and she knows not to pull.

FOLLOWING

Start by training your dog to follow you. Many puppies will follow if you simply walk away from them and maybe click your fingers or chuckle. Adult dogs may require additional enticement to stimulate them to follow, such as a training lure or, at the very least, a lively trainer. To teach the dog to follow: (1) keep walking and (2) walk away from the dog. If the dog attempts to lead or lag, change pace; slow down if the dog forges too far ahead, but speed up if she lags too far behind. Say "Steady!" or "Easy!" each time before you slow down and "Quickly!" or "Hustle!" each time before you speed up, and the dog will learn to change pace on cue. If the dog lags or leads too far, or if she wanders right or left, simply walk quickly in the opposite direction and maybe even run away from the dog and hide.

Practicing is a lot of fun; you can set up a course in your home, yard or park to do this. Indoors, entice the dog to follow upstairs, into a bedroom, into the bathroom, downstairs, around the living room couch, zigzagging between dining room chairs and into the kitchen for dinner. Outdoors, get the dog to follow around park benches, trees, shrubs and along walkways and lines in the grass. (For safety outdoors, it is advisable to attach a long line on the dog, but never exert corrective tension on the line.)

Remember, following has a lot to do with attitude—
your attitude! Most probably your dog will *not* want to
follow Mr. Grumpy Troll with the personality of wilted
lettuce. Lighten up—walk with a jaunty step, whistle a
happy tune, sing, skip and tell jokes to your dog and
she will be right there by your side.

BY YOUR SIDE

It is smart to train the dog to walk close on one side or
the other—either side will do, your choice. When walking, jogging or cycling, it is generally bad news to have
the dog suddenly cut in front of you. In fact, I train my
dogs to walk "By my side" and "Other side"—both very
useful instructions. It is possible to position the dog
fairly accurately by looking to the appropriate side and
clicking your fingers or slapping your thigh on that
side. A precise positioning may be attained by holding
a training lure, such as a chew toy, tennis ball or food
treat. Stop and stand still several times throughout the
walk, just as you would when window shopping or
meeting a friend. Use the lure to make sure the dog
slows down and stays close whenever you stop.

When teaching the dog to heel, we generally want
her to sit in heel position when we stop. Teach heel

Using a toy to teach sit-heel-sit sequences: 1) "Phoenix, sit!" Standing still, move lure up and back over dog's muzzle . . . 2) to position dog sitting in heel position on your left side. 3) Say "Phoenix, heel!" and walk ahead, wagging lure in left hand. Change lure to right hand in preparation for sit signal. Say "Sit" and then . . .

position at the standstill and the dog will learn that the default heel position is sitting by your side (left or right—your choice, unless you wish to compete in obedience trials, in which case the dog must heel on the left).

Several times a day, stand up and call your dog to come and sit in heel position—"Tina, heel!" For example, instruct the dog to come to heel each time there are commercials on TV, or each time you turn a page of a novel, and the dog will get it in a single evening.

Practice straight-line heeling and turns separately. With the dog sitting at heel, teach her to turn in place. After each quarter-turn, half-turn or full turn in place, lure the dog to sit at heel. Now it's time for short straight-line heeling sequences, no more than a few steps at a time. Always think of heeling in terms of sit-heel-sit sequences—start and end with the dog in position and do your best to keep her there when moving. Progressively increase the number of steps in each sequence. When the dog remains close for 20 yards of straight-line heeling, it is time to add a few turns and then sign up for a happy-heeling obedience class to get some advice from the experts.

4) use hand signal to lure dog to sit as you stop. Eventually, dog will sit automatically at heel whenever you stop. 5) "Good dog!"

No Pulling on Leash

You can start teaching your dog not to pull on leash anywhere—in front of the television or outdoors—but regardless of location, you must not take a single step with tension in the leash. For a reason known only to dogs, even just a couple of paces of pulling on leash is intrinsically motivating and diabolically rewarding. Instead, attach the leash to the dog's collar, grasp the other end firmly with both hands held close to your chest, and stand still—do not budge an inch. Have somebody watch you with a stopwatch to time your progress, or else you will never believe this will work and so you will not even try the exercise, and your shoulder and the dog's neck will be traumatized for years to come.

Stand still and wait for the dog to stop pulling, and to sit and/or lie down. All dogs stop pulling and sit eventually. Most take only a couple of minutes; the all-time record is 22½ minutes. Time how long it takes. Gently praise the dog when she stops pulling, and as soon as she sits, enthusiastically praise the dog and take just one step forward, then immediately stand still. This single step usually demonstrates the ballistic reinforcing nature of pulling on leash; most dogs explode to the end of the leash, so be prepared for the strain. Stand firm and wait for the dog to sit again. Repeat this half a dozen times and you will probably notice a progressive reduction in the force of the dog's one-step explosions and a radical reduction in the time it takes for the dog to sit each time.

As the dog learns "Sit we go" and "Pull we stop," she will begin to walk forward calmly with each single step and automatically sit when you stop. Now try two steps before you stop. Wooooooo! Scary! When the dog has mastered two steps at a time, try for three. After each success, progressively increase the number of steps in the sequence: try four steps and then six, eight, ten and twenty steps before stopping. Congratulations! You are now walking the dog on leash.

Whenever walking with the dog (off leash or on leash), make sure you stop periodically to practice a few position commands and stays before instructing the dog to "Walk on!" (Remember, you want the dog to be compliant everywhere, not just in the kitchen when her dinner is at hand.) For example, stopping every 25 yards to briefly train the dog amounts to over 200 training interludes within a single 3-mile stroll. And each training session is in a different location. You will not believe the improvement within just the first mile of the first walk.

To put it another way, integrating training into a walk offers 200 separate opportunities to use the continuance of the walk as a reward to reinforce the dog's education. Moreover, some training interludes may comprise continuing education for the dog's walking skills: Alternate short periods of the dog walking calmly by your side with periods when the dog is allowed to sniff and investigate the environment. Now sniffing odors on the grass and meeting other dogs become rewards which reinforce the dog's calm and mannerly demeanor. Good Lord! Whatever next? Many enjoyable walks together of course. Happy trails!

THE IMPORTANCE OF TRICKS

Nothing will improve a dog's quality of life better than having a few tricks under her belt. Teaching any trick expands the dog's vocabulary, which facilitates communication and improves the owner's control. Also, specific tricks help prevent and resolve specific behavior problems. For example, by teaching the dog to fetch her toys, the dog learns carrying a toy makes the owner happy and, therefore, will be more likely to chew her toy than other inappropriate items.

More important, teaching tricks prompts owners to lighten up and train with a sunny disposition. Really, tricks should be no different from any other behaviors we put on cue. But they are. When teaching tricks, owners have a much sweeter attitude, which in turn motivates the dog and improves her willingness to comply. The dog feels tricks are a blast, but formal commands are a drag. In fact, tricks are so enjoyable, they may be used as rewards in training by asking the dog to come, sit and down-stay and then rollover for a tummy rub. Go on, try it: Crack a smile and even giggle when the dog promptly and willingly lies down and stays.

Most important, performing tricks prompts onlookers to smile and giggle. Many people are scared of dogs, especially large ones. And nothing can be more off-putting for a dog than to be constantly confronted by strangers who don't like her because of her size or the way she looks. Uneasy people put the dog on edge, causing her to back off and bark, only frightening people all the more. And so a vicious circle develops, with the people's fear fueling the dog's fear *and vice versa*. Instead, tie a pink ribbon to your dog's collar and practice all sorts of tricks on walks and in the park, and you will be pleasantly amazed how it changes people's attitudes toward your friendly dog. The dog's repertoire of tricks is limited only by the trainer's imagination. Below I have described three of my favorites:

SPEAK AND SHUSH

The training sequence involved in teaching a dog to bark on request is no different from that used when training any behavior on cue: request—lure—response—reward. As always, the secret of success lies in finding an effective lure. If the dog always barks at the doorbell, for example, say "Rover, speak!", have an accomplice ring the doorbell, then reward the dog for barking. After a few woofs, ask Rover to "Shush!", waggle a food treat under her nose (to entice her to sniff and thus to shush), praise her when quiet and eventually offer the treat as a reward. Alternate "Speak" and "Shush," progressively increasing the length of shush-time between each barking bout.

PLAY BOW

With the dog standing, say "Bow!" and lower the food lure (palm upwards) to rest between the dog's forepaws. Praise as the dog lowers her forequarters and sternum to the ground (as when teaching the down), but then lure the dog to stand and offer the treat. On successive trials, gradually increase the length of time the dog is required to remain in the play bow posture in order to gain a food reward. If the dog's rear end collapses into a down, say nothing and offer no reward; simply start over.

BE A BEAR

With the dog sitting backed into a corner to prevent her from toppling over backwards, say "Be a bear!" With bent paw and palm down, raise a lure upwards and backwards along the top of the dog's muzzle. Praise the dog when she sits up on her haunches and offer the treat as a reward. To prevent the dog from standing on her hind legs, keep the lure closer to the dog's muzzle. On each trial, progressively increase the length of time the dog is required to sit up to receive a food reward. Since lure-reward training is so easy, teach the dog to stand and walk on her hind legs as well!

Teaching "Be a Bear"

chapter 9

Getting
Active
with your Dog

by Bardi McLennan

Once you and your dog have graduated from basic obedience training and are beginning to work together as a team, you can take part in the growing world of dog activities. There are so many fun things to do with your dog! Just remember, people and dogs don't always learn at the same pace, so don't be upset if you (or your dog) need more than two basic training courses before your team becomes operational. Even smart dogs don't go straight to college from kindergarten!

Just as there are events geared to certain types of dogs, so there are ones that are more appealing to certain types of people. In some activities, you give the commands and your dog does the work (upland game hunting is one example), while in others, such as agility, you'll both get a workout. You may want to aim for prestigious titles to add to your dog's name, or you may want nothing more than the sheer enjoyment of being around other people and their dogs. Passive or active, participation has its own rewards.

Consider your dog's physical capabilities when looking into any of the canine activities. It's easy to see that a Basset Hound is not built for the racetrack, nor would a Chihuahua be the breed of choice for pulling a sled. A loyal dog will attempt almost anything you ask him to do, so it is up to you to know your

All dogs seem to love playing flyball.

dog's limitations. A dog must be physically sound in order to compete at any level in athletic activities, and being mentally sound is a definite plus. Advanced age, however, may not be a deterrent. Many dogs still hunt and herd at ten or twelve years of age. It's entirely possible for dogs to be "fit at 50." Take your dog for a checkup, explain to your vet the type of activity you have in mind and be guided by his or her findings.

You needn't be restricted to breed-specific sports if it's only fun you're after. Certain AKC activities are limited to designated breeds; however, as each new trial, test or sport has grown in popularity, so has the variety of breeds encouraged to participate at a fun level.

But don't shortchange your fun, or that of your dog, by thinking only of the basic function of her breed. Once a dog has learned how to learn, she can be taught to do just about anything as long as the size of the dog is right for the job and you both think it is fun and rewarding. In other words, you are a team.

To get involved in any of the activities detailed in this chapter, look for the names and addresses of the organizations that sponsor them in Chapter 13. You can also ask your breeder or a local dog trainer for contacts.

You can compete in obedience trials with a well trained dog.

Official American Kennel Club Activities

The following tests and trials are some of the events sanctioned by the AKC and sponsored by various dog clubs. Your dog's expertise will be rewarded with impressive titles. You can participate just for fun, or be competitive and go for those awards.

OBEDIENCE

Training classes begin with pups as young as three months of age in kindergarten puppy training, then advance to pre-novice (all exercises on lead) and go on to novice, which is where you'll start off-lead work. In obedience classes dogs learn to sit, stay, heel and come through a variety of exercises. Once you've got the basics down, you can enter obedience trials and work toward earning your dog's first degree, a C.D. (Companion Dog).

The next level is called "Open," in which jumps and retrieves perk up the dog's interest. Passing grades in competition at this level earn a C.D.X. (Companion Dog Excellent). Beyond that lies the goal of the most ambitious—Utility (U.D. and even U.D.X. or OTCh, an Obedience Champion).

AGILITY

All dogs can participate in the latest canine sport to have gained worldwide popularity for its fun and excitement, agility. It began in England as a canine version of horse show-jumping, but because dogs are more agile and able to perform on verbal commands, extra feats were added such as climbing, balancing and racing through tunnels or in and out of weave poles. Many of the obstacles (regulation or homemade) can be set up in your own backyard. If the agility bug bites, you could end up in international competition!

For starters, your dog should be obedience trained, even though, in the beginning, the lessons may all be taught on lead. Once the dog understands the commands (and you do, too), it's as easy as guiding the dog over a prescribed course, one obstacle at a time. In competition, the race is against the clock, so wear your running shoes! The dog starts with 200 points and the judge deducts for infractions and misadventures along the way.

All dogs seem to love agility and respond to it as if they were being turned loose in a playground paradise. Your dog's enthusiasm will be contagious; agility turns into great fun for dog and owner.

FIELD TRIALS AND HUNTING TESTS

There are field trials and hunting tests for the sporting breeds—retrievers, spaniels and pointing breeds, and for some hounds—Bassets, Beagles and Dachshunds. Field trials are competitive events that test a dog's ability to perform the functions for which she was bred. Hunting tests, which are open to retrievers,

---

TITLES AWARDED BY THE AKC

Conformation: Ch. (Champion)

Obedience: CD (Companion Dog); CDX (Companion Dog Excellent); UD (Utility Dog); UDX (Utility Dog Excellent); OTCh. (Obedience Trial Champion)

Field: JH (Junior Hunter); SH (Senior Hunter); MH (Master Hunter); AFCh. (Amateur Field Champion); FCh. (Field Champion)

Lure Coursing: JC (Junior Courser); SC (Senior Courser)

Herding: HT (Herding Tested); PT (Pre-Trial Tested); HS (Herding Started); HI (Herding Intermediate); HX (Herding Excellent); HCh. (Herding Champion)

Tracking: TD (Tracking Dog); TDX (Tracking Dog Excellent)

Agility: NAD (Novice Agility); OAD (Open Agility); ADX (Agility Excellent); MAX (Master Agility)

Earthdog Tests: JE (Junior Earthdog); SE (Senior Earthdog); ME (Master Earthdog)

Canine Good Citizen: CGC

Combination: DC (Dual Champion—Ch. and Fch.); TC (Triple Champion—Ch., Fch., and OTCh.)

spaniels and pointing breeds only, are noncompetitive and are a means of judging the dog's ability as well as that of the handler.

Hunting is a very large and complex part of canine sports, and if you own one of the breeds that hunts, the events are a great treat for your dog and you. He gets to do what he was bred for, and you get to work with him and watch him do it. You'll be proud of and amazed at what your dog can do.

Fortunately, the AKC publishes a series of booklets on these events, which outline the rules and regulations and include a glossary of the sometimes complicated terms. The AKC also publishes newsletters for field trialers and hunting test enthusiasts. The United Kennel Club (UKC) also has informative materials for the hunter and his dog.

Retrievers and other sporting breeds get to do what they're bred to in hunting tests.

HERDING TESTS AND TRIALS

Herding, like hunting, dates back to the first known uses man made of dogs. The interest in herding today is widespread, and if you own a herding breed, you can join in the activity. Herding dogs are tested for their natural skills to keep a flock of ducks, sheep or cattle together. If your dog shows potential, you can start at the testing level, where your dog can earn a title for showing an inherent herding ability. With training you can advance to the trial level, where your dog should be capable of controlling even difficult livestock in diverse situations.

LURE COURSING

The AKC Tests and Trials for Lure Coursing are open to traditional sighthounds—Greyhounds, Whippets,

Borzoi, Salukis, Afghan Hounds, Ibizan Hounds and Scottish Deerhounds—as well as to Basenjis and Rhodesian Ridgebacks. Hounds are judged on overall ability, follow, speed, agility and endurance. This is possibly the most exciting of the trials for spectators, because the speed and agility of the dogs is awesome to watch as they chase the lure (or "course") in heats of two or three dogs at a time.

TRACKING

Tracking is another activity in which almost any dog can compete because every dog that sniffs the ground when taken outdoors is, in fact, tracking. The hard part comes when the rules as to what, when and where the dog tracks are determined by a person, not the dog! Tracking tests cover a large area of fields, woods and roads. The tracks are laid hours before the dogs go to work on them, and include "tricks" like cross-tracks and sharp turns. If you're interested in search-and-rescue work, this is the place to start.

This tracking dog is hot on the trail.

EARTHDOG TESTS FOR SMALL TERRIERS AND DACHSHUNDS

These tests are open to Australian, Bedlington, Border, Cairn, Dandie Dinmont, Smooth and Wire Fox, Lakeland, Norfolk, Norwich, Scottish, Sealyham, Skye, Welsh and West Highland White Terriers as well as Dachshunds. The dogs need no prior training for this terrier sport. There is a qualifying test on the day of the event, so dog and handler learn the rules on the spot. These tests, or "digs," sometimes end with informal races in the late afternoon.

Here are some of the extracurricular obedience and racing activities that are not regulated by the AKC or UKC, but are generally run by clubs or a group of dog fanciers and are often open to all.

Canine Freestyle This activity is something new on the scene and is variously likened to dancing, dressage or ice skating. It is meant to show the athleticism of the dog, but also requires showmanship on the part of the dog's handler. If you and your dog like to ham it up for friends, you might want to look into freestyle.

Lure coursing lets sighthounds do what they do best—run!

Scent Hurdle Racing Scent hurdle racing is purely a fun activity sponsored by obedience clubs with members forming competing teams. The height of the hurdles is based on the size of the shortest dog on the team. On a signal, one team dog is released on each of two side-by-side courses and must clear every hurdle before picking up its own dumbbell from a platform and returning over the jumps to the handler. As each dog returns, the next on that team is sent. Of course, that is what the dogs are supposed to do. When the dogs improvise (going under or around the hurdles, stealing another dog's dumbbell, and so forth), it no doubt frustrates the handlers, but just adds to the fun for everyone else.

Flyball This type of racing is similar, but after negotiating the four hurdles, the dog comes to a flyball box, steps on a lever that releases a tennis ball into the air, catches the ball and returns over the hurdles to the starting point. This game also becomes extremely fun for spectators because the dogs sometimes cheat by catching a ball released by the dog in the next lane. Three titles can be earned—Flyball Dog (F.D.), Flyball Dog Excellent (F.D.X.) and Flyball Dog Champion (Fb.D.Ch.)—all awarded by the North American Flyball Association, Inc.

Dogsledding The name conjures up the Rocky Mountains or the frigid North, but you can find dogsled clubs in such unlikely spots as Maryland, North Carolina and Virginia! Dogsledding is primarily for the Nordic breeds such as the Alaskan Malamutes, Siberian Huskies and Samoyeds, but other breeds can try. There are some practical backyard applications to this sport, too. With parental supervision, almost any strong dog could pull a child's sled.

Coming over the A-frame on an agility course.

These are just some of the many recreational ways you can get to know and understand your multifaceted dog better and have fun doing it.

chapter 10

Your Dog
and your
Family

by Bardi McLennan

Adding a dog automatically increases your family by one, no matter whether you live alone in an apartment or are part of a mother, father and six kids household. The single-person family is fair game for numerous and varied canine misconceptions as to who is dog and who pays the bills, whereas a dog in a houseful of children will consider himself to be just one of the gang, littermates all. One dog and one child may give a dog reason to believe they are both kids or both dogs. Either interpretation requires parental supervision and sometimes speedy intervention.

As soon as one paw goes through the door into your home, Rufus (or Rufina) has to make many adjustments to become a part of your family. Your job is to make him fit in as painlessly as possible. An older dog may have some frame of reference from past experience, but to a 10-week-old puppy, everything is brand new: people, furniture, stairs, when and where people eat, sleep or watch TV, his own place and everyone else's space, smells, sounds, outdoors—everything!

Puppies, and newly acquired dogs of any age, do not need what we think of as "freedom." If you leave a new dog or puppy loose in the house, you will almost certainly return to chaotic destruction and the dog will forever after equate your homecoming with a time of punishment to be dreaded. It is unfair to give your dog what amounts to "freedom to get into trouble." Instead, confine him to a crate for brief periods of your absence (up to three or four hours) and, for the long haul, a workday for example, confine him to one untrashable area with his own toys, a bowl of water and a radio left on (low) in another room.

Lots of pets get along with each other just fine.

For the first few days, when not confined, put Rufus on a long leash tied to your wrist or waist. This umbilical cord method enables the dog to learn all about you from your body language and voice, and to learn by his own actions which things in the house are NO! and which ones are rewarded by "Good dog." House-training will be easier with the pup always by your side. Speaking of which, accidents do happen. That goal of "completely housetrained" takes up to a year, or the length of time it takes the pup to mature.

The All-Adult Family

Most dogs in an adults-only household today are likely to be latchkey pets, with no one home all day but the dog. When you return after a tough day on the job, the dog can and should be your relaxation therapy. But going home can instead be a daily frustration.

Separation anxiety is a very common problem for the dog in a working household. It may begin with whines and barks of loneliness, but it will soon escalate into a frenzied destruction derby. That is why it is so important to set aside the time to teach a dog to relax when left alone in his confined area and to understand that he can trust you to return.

Let the dog get used to your work schedule in easy stages. Confine him to one room and go in and out of that room over and over again. Be casual about it. No physical, voice or eye contact. When the pup no longer even notices your comings and goings, leave the house for varying lengths of time, returning to stay home for a few minutes and gradually increasing the time away. This training can take days, but the dog is learning that you haven't left him forever and that he can trust you.

Any time you leave the dog, but especially during this training period, be casual about your departure. No anxiety-building fond farewells. Just "Bye" and go! Remember the "Good dog" when you return to find everything more or less as you left it.

If things are a mess (or even a disaster) when you return, greet the dog, take him outside to eliminate, and then put him in his crate while you clean up. Rant and rave in the shower! *Do not* punish the dog. You were not there when it happened, and the rule is: Only punish as you catch the dog in the act of wrongdoing. Obviously, it makes sense to get your latchkey puppy when you'll have a week or two to spend on these training essentials.

Family weekend activities should include Rufus whenever possible. Depending on the pup's age, now is the time for a long walk in the park, playtime in the backyard, a hike in the woods. Socializing is as important as health care, good food and physical exercise, so visiting Aunt Emma or Uncle Harry and the next-door neighbor's dog or cat is essential to developing an out-going, friendly temperament in your pet.

If you are a single adult, socializing Rufus at home and away will prevent him from becoming overly protective of you (or just overly attached) and will also prevent such behavioral problems as dominance or fear of strangers.

Babies

Whether already here or on the way, babies figure larger than life in the eyes of a dog. If the dog is there first, let him in on all your baby preparations in the house. When baby arrives, let Rufus sniff any item of clothing that has been on the baby before Junior comes home. Then let Mom greet the dog first before introducing the new family member. Hold the baby down for the dog to see and sniff, but make sure some-one's holding the dog on lead in case of any sudden moves. Don't play keep-away or tease the dog with the baby, which only invites undesirable jump-ing up.

The dog and the baby are "family," and for starters can be treated almost as equals. Things rapidly change, however, espe-cially when baby takes to creeping around on all fours on the dog's turf or, better yet, has yummy pudding all over her face and hands! That's when a lot of things in the dog's and baby's lives become more separate than equal.

Dogs are perfect confidants.

Toddlers make terrible dog owners, but if you can't avoid the combination, use patient discipline (that is, positive teaching rather than punishment), and use time-outs before you run out of patience.

139

A dog and a baby (or toddler, or an assertive young child) should never be left alone together. Take the dog with you or confine him. With a baby or youngsters in the house, you'll have plenty of use for that wonderful canine safety device called a crate!

Young Children

Any dog in a house with kids will behave pretty much as the kids do, good or bad. But even good dogs and good children can get into trouble when play becomes rowdy and active.

Teach children how to play nicely with a puppy.

Legs bobbing up and down, shrill voices screeching, a ball hurtling overhead, all add up to exuberant frustration for a dog who's just trying to be part of the gang. In a pack of puppies, any legs or toys being chased would be caught by a set of teeth, and all the pups involved would understand that is how the game is played. Kids do not understand this, nor do parents tolerate it. Bring Rufus indoors before you have reason to regret it. This is time-out, not a punishment.

You can explain the situation to the children and tell them they must play quieter games until the puppy learns not to grab them with his mouth. Unfortunately, you can't explain it that easily to the dog. With adult supervision, they will learn how to play together.

Young children love to tease. Sticking their faces or wiggling their hands or fingers in the dog's face is teasing. To another person it might be just annoying, but it is threatening to a dog. There's another difference: We can make the child stop by an explanation, but the only way a dog can stop it is with a warning growl and then with teeth. Teasing is the major cause of children being bitten by their pets. Treat it seriously.

Older Children

The best age for a child to get a first dog is between the ages of 8 and 12. That's when kids are able to accept some real responsibility for their pet. Even so, take the child's vow of "I will never *ever* forget to feed (brush, walk, etc.) the dog" for what it's worth: a child's good intention at that moment. Most kids today have extra lessons, soccer practice, Little League, ballet, and so forth piled on top of school schedules. There will be many times when Mom will have to come to the dog's rescue. "I walked the dog for you so you can set the table for me" is one way to get around a missed appointment without laying on blame or guilt.

Kids in this age group make excellent obedience trainers because they are into the teaching/learning process themselves and they lack the self-consciousness of adults. Attending a dog show is something the whole family can enjoy, and watching Junior Showmanship may catch the eye of the kids. Older children can begin to get involved in many of the recreational activities that were reviewed in the previous chapter. Some of the agility obstacles, for example, can be set up in the backyard as a family project (with an adult making sure all the equipment is safe and secure for the dog).

Older kids are also beginning to look to the future, and may envision themselves as veterinarians or trainers or show dog handlers or writers of the next Lassie best-seller. Dogs are perfect confidants for these dreams. They won't tell a soul.

Other Pets

Introduce all pets tactfully. In a dog/cat situation, hold the dog, not the cat. Let two dogs meet on neutral turf—a stroll in the park or a walk down the street—with both on loose leads to permit all the normal canine ways of saying hello, including routine sniffing, circling, more sniffing, and so on. Small creatures such as hamsters, chinchillas or mice must be kept safe from their natural predators (dogs and cats).

Festive Family Occasions

Parties are great for people, but not necessarily for puppies. Until all the guests have arrived, put the dog in his crate or in a room where he won't be disturbed. A socialized dog can join the fun later as long as he's not underfoot, annoying guests or into the hors d'oeuvres.

There are a few dangers to consider, too. Doors opening and closing can allow a puppy to slip out unnoticed in the confusion, and you'll be organizing a search party instead of playing host or hostess. Party food and buffet service are not for dogs. Let Rufus party in his crate with a nice big dog biscuit.

At Christmas time, not only are tree decorations dangerous and breakable (and perhaps family heirlooms), but extreme caution should be taken with the lights, cords and outlets for the tree lights and any other festive lighting. Occasionally a dog lifts a leg, ignoring the fact that the tree is indoors. To avoid this, use a canine repellent, made for gardens, on the tree. Or keep him out of the tree room unless supervised. And whatever you do, *don't* invite trouble by hanging his toys on the tree!

Car Travel

Before you plan a vacation by car or RV with Rufus, be sure he enjoys car travel. Nothing spoils a holiday quicker than a carsick dog! Work within the dog's comfort level. Get in the car with the dog in his crate or attached to a canine car safety belt and just sit there until he relaxes. That's all. Next time, get in the car, turn on the engine and go nowhere. Just sit. When that is okay, turn on the engine and go around the block. Now you can go for a ride and include a stop where you get out, leaving the dog for a minute or two.

On a warm day, always park in the shade and leave windows open several inches. And return quickly. It only takes 10 minutes for a car to become an overheated steel death trap.

Motel or Pet Motel?

Not all motels or hotels accept pets, but you have a much better choice today than even a few years ago. To find a dog-friendly lodging, look at *On the Road Again With Man's Best Friend*, a series of directories that detail bed and breakfasts, inns, family resorts and other hotels/motels. Some places require a refundable deposit to cover any damage incurred by the dog. More B&Bs accept pets now, but some restrict the size.

If taking Rufus with you is not feasible, check out boarding kennels in your area. Your veterinarian may offer this service, or recommend a kennel or two he or she is familiar with. Go see the facilities for yourself, ask about exercise, diet, housing, and so on. Or, if you'd rather have Rufus stay home, look into bonded petsitters, many of whom will also bring in the mail and water your plants.

chapter 11

Your Dog
and your
Community

by Bardi McLennan

Step outside your home with your dog and you are no longer just family, you are both part of your community. This is when the phrase "responsible pet ownership" takes on serious implications. For starters, it means you pick up after your dog—not just occasionally, but every time your dog eliminates away from home. That means you have joined the Plastic Baggy Brigade! You always have plastic sandwich bags in your pocket and several in the car. It means you teach your kids how to use them, too. If you think this is "yucky," just imagine what the person (a non-doggy person) who inadvertently steps in the mess thinks!

Your responsibility extends to your neighbors: To their ears (no annoying barking); to their property (their garbage, their lawn, their flower beds, their cat— especially their cat); to their kids (on bikes, at play); to their kids' toys and sports equipment.

There are numerous dog-related laws, ranging from simple dog licensing and leash laws to those holding you liable for any physical injury or property damage done by your dog. These laws are in place to protect everyone in the community, including you and your dog. There are town ordinances and state laws which are by no means the same in all towns or all states. Ignorance of the law won't get you off the hook. The time to find out what the laws are where you live is now.

Be sure your dog's license is current. This is not just a good local ordinance, it can make the difference between finding your lost dog or not.

Dressing your dog up makes him appealing to strangers.

Many states now require proof of rabies vaccination and that the dog has been spayed or neutered before issuing a license. At the same time, keep up the dog's annual immunizations.

Never let your dog run loose in the neighborhood. This will not only keep you, on the right side of the leash law, it's the outdoor version of the rule about not giving your dog "freedom to get into trouble."

Good Canine Citizen

Sometimes it's hard for a dog's owner to assess whether or not the dog is sufficiently socialized to be accepted by the community at large. Does Rufus or Rufina display good, controlled behavior in public? The AKC's Canine Good Citizen program is available through many dog organizations. If your dog passes the test, the title "CGC" is earned.

The overall purpose is to turn your dog into a good neighbor and to teach you about your responsibility to your community as a dog owner. Here are the ten things your dog must do willingly:

1. Accept a stranger stopping to chat with you.
2. Sit and be petted by a stranger.
3. Allow a stranger to handle him or her as a groomer or veterinarian would.
4. Walk nicely on a loose lead.
5. Walk calmly through a crowd.
6. Sit and down on command, then stay in a sit or down position while you walk away.
7. Come when called.
8. Casually greet another dog.
9. React confidently to distractions.
10. Accept being left alone with someone other than you and not become overly agitated or nervous.

Schools and Dogs

Schools are getting involved with pet ownership on an educational level. It has been proven that children who are kind to animals are humane in their attitude toward other people as adults.

A dog is a child's best friend, and so children are often primary pet owners, if not the primary caregivers. Unfortunately, they are also the ones most often bitten by dogs. This occurs due to a lack of understanding that pets, no matter how sweet, cuddly and loving, are still animals. Schools, along with parents, dog clubs, dog fanciers and the AKC, are working to change all that with video programs for children not only in grade school, but in the nursery school and pre-kindergarten age group. Teaching youngsters how to be responsible dog owners is important community work. When your dog has a CGC, volunteer to take part in an educational classroom event put on by your dog club.

Boy Scout Merit Badge

A Merit Badge for Dog Care can be earned by any Boy
Scout ages 11 to 18. The requirements are not easy, but
amount to a complete course in responsible dog care
and general ownership. Here are just a few of the
things a Scout must do to earn that badge:

Point out ten parts of the dog using the correct
names.

Give a report (signed by parent or guardian) on
your care of the dog (feeding, food used, housing,
exercising, grooming and bathing), plus what has
been done to keep the dog healthy.

Explain the right way to obedience train a dog,
and demonstrate three comments.

Several of the requirements have to do with health
care, including first aid, handling a hurt dog, and
the dangers of home treatment for a serious
ailment.

The final requirement is to know the local laws
and ordinances involving dogs.

There are similar programs for Girl Scouts and 4-H
members.

Local Clubs

Local dog clubs are no longer in existence just to put
on a yearly dog show. Today, they are apt to be the hub
of the community's involvement with pets. Dog clubs
conduct educational forums with big-name speakers,
stage demonstrations of canine talent in a busy mall
and take dogs of various breeds to schools for classroom discussion.

The quickest way to feel accepted as a member in a
club is to volunteer your services! Offer to help with
something—anything—and watch your popularity
(and your interest) grow.

Therapy Dogs

Once your dog has earned that essential CGC and reliably demonstrates a steady, calm temperament, you could look into what therapy dogs are doing in your area.

Therapy dogs go with their owners to visit patients at hospitals or nursing homes, generally remaining on leash but able to coax a pat from a stiffened hand, a smile from a blank face, a few words from sealed lips or a hug from someone in need of love.

Nursing homes cover a wide range of patient care. Some specialize in care of the elderly, some in the treatment of specific illnesses, some in physical therapy. Children's facilities also welcome visits from trained therapy dogs for boosting morale in their pediatric patients. Hospice care for the terminally ill and the at-home care of AIDS patients are other areas where this canine visiting is desperately needed. Therapy dog training comes first.

Your dog can make a difference in lots of lives.

There is a lot more involved than just taking your nice friendly pooch to someone's bedside. Doing therapy dog work involves your own emotional stability as well as that of your dog. But once you have met all the requirements for this work, making the rounds once a week or once a month with your therapy dog is possibly the most rewarding of all community activities.

Disaster Aid

This community service is definitely not for everyone, partly because it is time-consuming. The initial training is rigorous, and there can be no let-up in the continuing workouts, because members are on call 24 hours a day to go wherever they are needed at a moment's notice. But if you think you would like to be able to assist in a disaster, look into search-and-rescue work. The network of search-and-rescue volunteers is worldwide, and all members of the American Rescue Dog Association (ARDA) who are qualified to do this work are volunteers who train and maintain their own dogs.

Physical Aid

Most people are familiar with Seeing Eye dogs, which serve as blind people's eyes, but not with all the other work that dogs are trained to do to assist the disabled. Dogs are also specially trained to pull wheelchairs, carry school books, pick up dropped objects, open and close doors. Some also are ears for the deaf. All these assistance-trained dogs, by the way, are allowed anywhere "No Pet" signs exist (as are therapy dogs when

Making the rounds with your therapy dog can be very rewarding.

properly identified). Getting started in any of this fascinating work requires a background in dog training and canine behavior, but there are also volunteer jobs ranging from answering the phone to cleaning out kennels to providing a foster home for a puppy. You have only to ask.

part four

Beyond
the
Basics

chapter 12

Recommended Reading

Books

ABOUT HEALTH CARE

Ackerman, Lowell. *Guide to Skin and Haircoat Problems in Dogs.* Loveland, Colo.: Alpine Publications, 1994.

Alderton, David. *The Dog Care Manual.* Hauppauge, N.Y.: Barron's Educational Series, Inc., 1986.

American Kennel Club. *American Kennel Club Dog Care and Training.* New York: Howell Book House, 1991.

Bamberger, Michelle, DVM. *Help! The Quick Guide to First Aid for Your Dog.* New York: Howell Book House, 1995.

Carlson, Delbert, DVM, and James Giffin, MD. *Dog Owner's Home Veterinary Handbook.* New York: Howell Book House, 1992.

DeBitetto, James, DVM, and Sarah Hodgson. *You & Your Puppy.* New York: Howell Book House, 1995.

Humphries, Jim, DVM. *Dr. Jim's Animal Clinic for Dogs.* New York: Howell Book House, 1994.

McGinnis, Terri. *The Well Dog Book.* New York: Random House, 1991.

Pitcairn, Richard and Susan. *Natural Health for Dogs.* Emmaus, Pa.: Rodale Press, 1982.

ABOUT DOG SHOWS

Hall, Lynn. *Dog Showing for Beginners.* New York: Howell Book House, 1994.

Nichols, Virginia Tuck. *How to Show Your Own Dog.* Neptune, N. J.: TFH, 1970.

Vanacore, Connie. *Dog Showing, An Owner's Guide.* New York: Howell Book House, 1990.

About Training

Ammen, Amy. *Training in No Time*. New York: Howell Book House, 1995.

Baer, Ted. *Communicating With Your Dog*. Hauppauge, N.Y.: Barron's Educational Series, Inc., 1989.

Benjamin, Carol Lea. *Dog Problems*. New York: Howell Book House, 1989.

Benjamin, Carol Lea. *Dog Training for Kids*. New York: Howell Book House, 1988.

Benjamin, Carol Lea. *Mother Knows Best*. New York: Howell Book House, 1985.

Benjamin, Carol Lea. *Surviving Your Dog's Adolescence*. New York: Howell Book House, 1993.

Bohnenkamp, Gwen. *Manners for the Modern Dog*. San Francisco: Perfect Paws, 1990.

Dibra, Bashkim. *Dog Training by Bash*. New York: Dell, 1992.

Dunbar, Ian, PhD, MRCVS. *Dr. Dunbar's Good Little Dog Book*, James & Kenneth Publishers, 2140 Shattuck Ave. #2406, Berkeley, Calif. 94704. (510) 658–8588. Order from the publisher.

Dunbar, Ian, PhD, MRCVS. *How to Teach a New Dog Old Tricks*, James & Kenneth Publishers. Order from the publisher; address above.

Dunbar, Ian, PhD, MRCVS, and Gwen Bohnenkamp. Booklets on *Preventing Aggression; Housetraining; Chewing; Digging; Barking; Socialization; Fearfulness; and Fighting*, James & Kenneth Publishers. Order from the publisher; address above.

Evans, Job Michael. *People, Pooches and Problems*. New York: Howell Book House, 1991.

Kilcommons, Brian and Sarah Wilson. *Good Owners, Great Dogs*. New York: Warner Books, 1992.

McMains, Joel M. *Dog Logic—Companion Obedience*. New York: Howell Book House, 1992.

Rutherford, Clarice and David H. Neil, MRCVS. *How to Raise a Puppy You Can Live With*. Loveland, Colo.: Alpine Publications, 1982.

Volhard, Jack and Melissa Bartlett. *What All Good Dogs Should Know: The Sensible Way to Train*. New York: Howell Book House, 1991.

About Breeding

Harris, Beth J. Finder. *Breeding a Litter, The Complete Book of Prenatal and Postnatal Care*. New York: Howell Book House, 1983.

Holst, Phyllis, DVM. *Canine Reproduction*. Loveland, Colo.: Alpine Publications, 1985.

Walkowicz, Chris and Bonnie Wilcox, DVM. *Successful Dog Breeding, The Complete Handbook of Canine Midwifery.* New York: Howell Book House, 1994.

ABOUT ACTIVITIES

American Rescue Dog Association. *Search and Rescue Dogs.* New York: Howell Book House, 1991.

Barwig, Susan and Stewart Hilliard. *Schutzhund.* New York: Howell Book House, 1991.

Beaman, Arthur S. *Lure Coursing.* New York: Howell Book House, 1994.

Daniels, Julie. *Enjoying Dog Agility—From Backyard to Competition.* New York: Doral Publishing, 1990.

Davis, Kathy Diamond. *Therapy Dogs.* New York: Howell Book House, 1992.

Gallup, Davis Anne. *Running With Man's Best Friend.* Loveland, Colo.: Alpine Publications, 1986.

Habgood, Dawn and Robert. *On the Road Again With Man's Best Friend.* New England, Mid-Atlantic, West Coast and Southeast editions. Selective guides to area bed and breakfasts, inns, hotels and resorts that welcome guests and their dogs. New York: Howell Book House, 1995.

Holland, Vergil S. *Herding Dogs.* New York: Howell Book House, 1994.

LaBelle, Charlene G. *Backpacking With Your Dog.* Loveland, Colo.: Alpine Publications, 1993.

Simmons-Moake, Jane. *Agility Training, The Fun Sport for All Dogs.* New York: Howell Book House, 1991.

Spencer, James B. *Hup! Training Flushing Spaniels the American Way.* New York: Howell Book House, 1992.

Spencer, James B. *Point! Training the All-Seasons Birddog.* New York: Howell Book House, 1995.

Tarrant, Bill. *Training the Hunting Retriever.* New York: Howell Book House, 1991.

Volhard, Jack and Wendy. *The Canine Good Citizen.* New York: Howell Book House, 1994.

General Titles

Haggerty, Captain Arthur J. *How to Get Your Pet Into Show Business.* New York: Howell Book House, 1994.

McLennan, Bardi. *Dogs and Kids, Parenting Tips.* New York: Howell Book House, 1993.

Moran, Patti J. *Pet Sitting for Profit, A Complete Manual for Professional Success.* New York: Howell Book House, 1992.

Scalisi, Danny and Libby Moses. *When Rover Just Won't Do, Over 2,000 Suggestions for Naming Your Dog.* New York: Howell Book House, 1993.

Sife, Wallace, PhD. *The Loss of a Pet.* New York: Howell Book House, 1993.

Wrede, Barbara J. *Civilizing Your Puppy.* Hauppauge, N.Y.: Barron's Educational Series, 1992.

Magazines

The AKC GAZETTE, The Official Journal for the Sport of Purebred Dogs. American Kennel Club, 51 Madison Ave., New York, NY.

Bloodlines Journal. United Kennel Club, 100 E. Kilgore Rd., Kalamazoo, MI.

Dog Fancy. Fancy Publications, 3 Burroughs, Irvine, CA 92718

Dog World. Maclean Hunter Publishing Corp., 29 N. Wacker Dr., Chicago, IL 60606.

Videos

"SIRIUS Puppy Training," by Ian Dunbar, PhD, MRCVS. James & Kenneth Publishers, 2140 Shattuck Ave. #2406, Berkeley, CA 94704. Order from the publisher.

"Training the Companion Dog," from Dr. Dunbar's British TV Series, James & Kenneth Publishers. (See address above).

The American Kennel Club produces videos on every breed of dog, as well as on hunting tests, field trials and other areas of interest to purebred dog owners. For more information, write to AKC/Video Fulfillment, 5580 Centerview Dr., Suite 200, Raleigh, NC 27606.

Resources

chapter 13

Breed Clubs

Every breed recognized by the American Kennel Club has a national (parent) club. National clubs are a great source of information on your breed. You can get the name of the secretary of the club by contacting:

The American Kennel Club
51 Madison Avenue
New York, NY 10010
(212) 696-8200

There are also numerous all-breed, individual breed, obedience, hunting and other special-interest dog clubs across the country. The American Kennel Club can provide you with a geographical list of clubs to find ones in your area. Contact them at the above address.

Registry Organizations

Registry organizations register purebred dogs. The American Kennel Club is the oldest and largest in this country, and currently recognizes over 130 breeds. The United Kennel Club registers some breeds the AKC doesn't (including the American Pit Bull Terrier and the Miniature Fox Terrier) as well as many of the same breeds. The others included here are for your reference; the AKC can provide you with a list of foreign registries.

American Kennel Club
51 Madison Avenue
New York, NY 10010

United Kennel Club (UKC)
100 E. Kilgore Road
Kalamazoo, MI 49001-5598

American Dog Breeders Assn.
P.O. Box 1771
Salt Lake City, UT 84110
(Registers American Pit Bull Terriers)

Canadian Kennel Club
89 Skyway Avenue
Etobicoke, Ontario
Canada M9W 6R4

National Stock Dog Registry
P.O. Box 402
Butler, IN 46721
(Registers working stock dogs)

Orthopedic Foundation for Animals (OFA)
2300 E. Nifong Blvd.
Columbia, MO 65201-3856
(Hip registry)

Activity Clubs

Write to these organizations for information on the activities they sponsor.

American Kennel Club
51 Madison Avenue
New York, NY 10010
(Conformation Shows, Obedience Trials, Field Trials and Hunting Tests, Agility, Canine Good

Citizen, Lure Coursing, Herding, Tracking,
Earthdog Tests, Coonhunting.)

United Kennel Club
100 E. Kilgore Road
Kalamazoo, MI 49001-5598
(Conformation Shows, Obedience Trials, Agility,
Hunting for Various Breeds, Terrier Trials and
more.)

North American Flyball Assn.
1342 Jeff St.
Ypsilanti, MI 48198

International Sled Dog Racing Assn.
P.O. Box 446
Norman, ID 83848-0446

North American Working Dog Assn., Inc.
Southeast Kreisgruppe
P.O. Box 833
Brunswick, GA 31521

Trainers

Association of Pet Dog Trainers
P.O. Box 385
Davis, CA 95617
(800) PET–DOGS

American Dog Trainers' Network
161 West 4th St.
New York, NY 10014
(212) 727–7257

**National Association of Dog Obedience
Instructors**
2286 East Steel Rd.
St. Johns, MI 48879

Associations

American Dog Owners Assn.
1654 Columbia Tpk.
Castleton, NY 12033
(Combats anti-dog legislation)

Delta Society
P.O. Box 1080
Renton, WA 98057-1080
(Promotes the human/animal bond through
pet-assisted therapy and other programs)

Dog Writers Assn. of America (DWAA)
Sally Cooper, Secy.
222 Woodchuck Ln.
Harwinton, CT 06791

National Assn. for Search and Rescue (NASAR)
P.O. Box 3709
Fairfax, VA 22038

Therapy Dogs International
6 Hilltop Road
Mendham, NJ 07945